ROUTLEDGE LIBRARY EDITIONS:
ACCOUNTING

Volume 28

BUSINESS BUDGETS AND ACCOUNTS

BUSINESS BUDGETS AND ACCOUNTS

HAROLD C. EDEY

Routledge
Taylor & Francis Group

LONDON AND NEW YORK

First published in 1959

This edition first published in 2014
by Routledge
2 Park Square, Milton Park, Abingdon, Oxon, OX14 4RN

and by Routledge
711 Third Avenue, New York, NY 10017

Routledge is an imprint of the Taylor & Francis Group, an informa business

British Library Cataloguing in Publication Data
A catalogue record for this book is available from the British Library

ISBN: 978-0-415-53081-1 (Set)
eISBN: 978-1-315-88628-2 (Set)
ISBN: 978-0-415-70221-8 (Volume 28)
eISBN: 978-1-315-88337-3 (Volume 28)

Publisher's Note
The publisher has gone to great lengths to ensure the quality of this reprint but points out that some imperfections in the original copies may be apparent.

Disclaimer
The publisher has made every effort to trace copyright holders and would welcome correspondence from those they have been unable to trace.

PREFACE

This book has been written to show the relevance of accounting methods to the economic and administrative problems of business and, in so doing, to demonstrate the general nature of some of these. It will, I hope, be of value to accountants, economists, business men, and others interested in their problems. I should emphasize that it is not a treatise on accounting techniques and procedures, though I hope it may prove a useful introduction to the study of these, leading to an appreciation of the purposes they are intended to serve. For the economist it will provide, I hope, an aid in the study of the practice of the firm that is lacking in more general theoretical formulations.

The need for studies that relate economics and accounting to one another, and show the relevance of both to business applications, is becoming increasingly obvious at a time when exciting developments in electronics are bringing into the business world, and particularly into the field of accounting and business statistics generally, mathematicians, electrical engineers and others who have all too few texts to which to turn in order to find out what the business man and his accountants are getting at. For the same reason it is becoming increasingly important for accountants to develop a critical approach towards their hitherto too-seldom-questioned techniques and doctrines.

The book has been arranged to take the reader through the budgeting procedure of a representative—and imaginary—business, demonstrating the relationship between the budgets and accounts and the various business activities, and showing how the budgets and accounts link together the balance sheets at the beginning and end of the year.

My aim has been to demonstrate principles rather than to provide an exhaustive description of business. Needless to say, in an exposition confined to some 60,000 words selection is inevitable;

expert and thoughtful non-expert readers will find many matters omitted that another writer might have preferred to include. Nor, I suppose, will the arrangement of subject matter please everyone. Were I, now that I have completed the book, to rewrite it from the beginning, I should quite possibly change the arrangement. Perfect symmetry is, however, costly, both in space and in reader's time, and could hardly be obtained in so short a space without a serious reduction in content.

Such merit as the book has should be attributed in large measure to the intellectual stimulus of my colleagues at the London School of Economics, whom I take this opportunity of thanking collectively. I owe a debt to Sir Roy Harrod, who pointed out a number of defects in the original typescript, but who is, of course, in no way responsible for those that remain. I should also like to thank Miss Greta Bourke, who with great patience typed the half-legible drafts.

H. C. E.

concerns, net profit, is not the same as aim (*b*), the attainment of the required level of money at different points of time. A revenue or cost is a gain or sacrifice of value—money's worth: this may not be in the form of available money at all; a business that has made a profit in a given period and thereby increased the total value of its collection of resources may yet be short of ready money, and even be forced into bankruptcy because it is unable to find the cash to pay its debts as they fall due, so that, for example, other resources have to be sold rapidly at knock-down prices; and a business may make a loss at a time when it still holds a large cash balance at the bank. There is, however, a close connection between aims (*a*) and (*b*) in the longer run: a business whose costs persistently exceed its revenues must sooner or later run out of money; and on the other hand, a business that is consistently profitable will usually be able to obtain ready money fairly quickly by borrowing, or even by selling some of its non-money resources. There is also a continuing relationship between aims (*a*), (*b*) and (*c*), taken together, with which we shall become familiar as our study proceeds.

The accounting statement of the type that we call the income, or profit and loss, account, is devised to provide a classified analysis of the component revenues and costs that together make up the net profit for any given period. The net profit itself is a measure of the degree of success achieved in meeting whatever figure justifies the continued use in the business of the resources as a whole. We shall note in Chapter 10, after we have learnt more about the construction of the profit and loss statement and its components, some of the problems that arise in setting this target figure, which, indeed, often represents more a theoretical concept than a conscious idea in the mind of the business administrator; even when this is true, however, the profit (or loss) achieved, and the question whether this should have been greater or less, remains of fundamental importance.

The detailed analysis of the profit and loss components is a guide to the relative contributions, positive or negative, of the different activities carried on inside the business. The revenues and costs can be analysed in ways that correspond to the particular types of goods and services that have been absorbed in carrying on the business activities: the costs can be determined, for example, of using different kinds of raw materials for manufacture, of hiring particular kinds of labour, and so on. A well-constructed income account, with adequate supporting analysis extending to what is called 'cost accounting', can be a powerful engine of economic control, providing a detailed analysis of transactions that enables, within limits, the causes of the revenues and costs to be isolated and studied, and the interrelations between these to be examined, with the object of learning from the past how better results can be obtained in the future.

It is particularly important that the administrator of any business undertaking, or part of an undertaking, should be continually aware of the size of the inward and outward flow of money, and the quantity of ready money available at all points of time. This study of the 'liquidity' of the undertaking is almost impossible in all but the simplest business situations unless careful accounting records are maintained of the money flows. Businesses vary a good deal in the quality of their accounting systems and many small businesses have systems that provide much less information than would probably be useful; it is most unusual, however, to find any business that does not keep a fairly accurate record of its cash flows. The administrator must always be ready to take quick action if it should appear, from the trend in the flows, and from the information available about the probable flows in the near future, that there will not be enough ready money available to meet the debts that are falling due, or to take advantage of the business opportunities that appear likely to offer themselves.

The changes in the quantity of money held by the business are, by definition, dependent upon the changes in all the other assets and liabilities, both in form—that is, in the type of asset or liability —and in the total value. In our progress through the book we shall see how all the changes in the assets and liabilities, including money, interlock. This dependence of the inflow and outflow of money upon the set of assets of which a business disposes, and the liabilities, is one of the reasons why the asset structure must be kept under close watch. For example, the amount of debts that are owing to the business at any moment of time determines in part the amount of money that will shortly be collected, and the amount of short term liabilities from the business to outsiders determines the amounts of money that will shortly have to be paid out. The asset structure is earlier accounting reports, but often to a large degree based on a kind of *ad hoc* reasoning, mixed with intuition. There are considerable advantages to be gained by adopting a more systematic procedure, and an increasing number of businesses are finding that the use of budgets can provide an appropriate formal pattern. A budget, indeed, can be regarded as the statement of what an account is expected to look like after the events that have been planned for a given period have taken place. By taking carefully into account all the expected activities of the business, and considering the effect of these on the economic situation of the business, it is possible to construct estimates of the accounting results for various parts of the business and for the business as a whole. It is also possible, by careful study, to establish standard economic results that are expected to follow from particular sectional business operations, and these can be used in constructing the budgets and in interpreting the actual accounting results. The budgets, and the standards that they incorporate, can be regarded as the economic expression of hypotheses or 'theories' concerning the future behaviour of the business. Every plan made in business, and every action taken, assumes, explicitly or implicitly, the existence of relationships of some kind between the action planned and its economic results—that is, it assumes a set of hypotheses. It would be wrong to distinguish sharply between business activity and what is generally called scientific work. The business man, just like the scientist, has to make projections and take decisions on the basis of these.[1]

Thus, budgets can be used to assist in the economic control of business through the process of what is sometimes called 'budgetary control', that is, the constant checking of the actual accounting results against the original budgets with the object of detecting to what extent errors have been made, controlling the work of different members of the organization, and providing material for further forecasts about the future; the use of budgets and accounts in this way can be compared with the way in which a navigator plots a course and then uses the figures obtained from astronomical

[1] It is quite wrong to claim that business men are 'practical' as opposed to 'theoretical'. The hypotheses or theories they habitually employ require, on the contrary, such bold assumptions compared with those normally used by scientists that the latter ought to look on business men as the starriest-eyed visionaries.

observations and radar measurements to check his actual movements against the course he has plotted, and make appropriate amendments. Budgets have, however, other important contributions to make.

One of the advantages of budgeting that is very frequently emphasized is the fact that its exercise draws the attention of the administrators in a business more explicitly to the nature of the problems that are facing them, and leads to more careful and critical thinking, and greater precision. It improves control over subordinates, since their proposed actions can be budgeted and they can be asked to agree beforehand to these budgets so that, if later deviations from the budgeted figures are found, they can be reasonably asked for explanations. Budgets become particularly important when the degree of delegation is high and in particular where businesses are extensively split into divisions and sections. Where there is a high degree of delegation—and it is not possible to carry on large-scale enterprise without this—the problem of co-ordination becomes a very serious one. If there is insufficient or bad co-ordination the risk is increased that different sections of the organization will carry on activities that are mutually inconsistent. One of the important functions of budgets is to bring, so far as possible, the activities of the different parts of the business into a common, consistent, system. Furthermore, the budgets provide, so to speak, the operational plan of the business. Once they have been approved by the top members of the administrative hierarchy, everyone concerned knows, within limits, what he is expected to do, and in this way the general policy of whoever is in control of the business can be conveyed to all members of the staff.

Budgeting is also of importance in relation to the longer term plans of business. Even though no formal budgets may be prepared, it is impossible in practice to carry on business without making some kind of rough forecasts about the long term effect of current actions. Much business outlay is of a nature that will not be recovered for a number of years; when, for example, heavy plant and equipment is laid down, a hostage to fortune may be given for five, ten, fifteen or more years. The preparation of formal budgets imposes a discipline that may well lead to more careful and critical thinking about the future.

the choice of these five departments. In real life, again, the division of responsibility varies greatly from business to business. It would, for example, have been in no way unusual to divide the functions of production and purchasing into two departments, or to have a separate legal department, and so on. The choice here has been made arbitrarily and purely on grounds of convenience. The significance of the various departments—the work they do—will become apparent as we proceed.

In many businesses, particularly smaller ones, some, if not all, of the departmental managers would be members of the board of directors—so-called 'working directors'. Even if the office of director is combined with a managerial job, however, the two functions remain distinct. The sales manager who is also a director has two quite different kinds of job to do. As sales manager he is responsible for his department; as a director he is with his fellow directors responsible for the general control, on behalf of the shareholders, of the company. We separate these two functions in our discussion by assuming that in our representative company they are fulfilled by different people.

The division of responsibility between the board of directors and the general manager is not one about which definite rules can be laid down. It is often said that it is the function of the board to decide general policy—the general aims of the business. This, however, is merely to re-state the question in other words; it does not tell us the answer because 'general policy' has no definite meaning. Practice on this point varies widely. For our purpose it is enough to note that most boards of directors do in fact reserve certain stated matters for their own decision: the matters so reserved can if desired be called matters of general policy so far as *that* company is concerned.

The relationship between the board of directors and the shareholders is of importance in connection with the use of accounts for the control of directors, and for the valuation of businesses and interests in businesses—financial accounting. We shall be unable to consider these, however, in this book. We shall therefore assume that the interests of directors and shareholders are identical as, indeed, is often the case, for, particularly in small companies, the directors are often the sole shareholders.

2

THE ANNUAL BUDGETS

IT IS common practice to speak of 'the annual budget' of a business in the singular. The usual practice, however, is to have budgets for different activities of the business, corresponding to the divisions of managerial responsibility. These budgets provide the data for the general profit and loss budget, the finance budget (which records the planned flows of money into and out of the business), and the budgeted balance sheet at the end of the period, which sum up the planned economic results of the business as a whole.

Each budget expresses in money values the physical activities to which it relates.[1] Thus, the sales revenue budget shows the planned selling value of the goods to be sold, the production cost budget shows the value of the goods to be made, and so on. Different budgets could be drawn up for each of an indefinitely large number of alternative sets of business activities. The budgets actually adopted imply that the activities which they reflect, and upon which they are based, are those believed by the persons in control to be the best out of all those that have been taken into consideration.[2] The procedure of business budgeting might, therefore, be described in terms of setting up budgets for each possible alternative course of action, thus making explicit the expected economic effect—gain or loss and change in the form of the business resources—of each course, and then of selecting the set of budgets giving the best result, thereby determining the appropriate action. This is not a bad way of looking at business behaviour, because it draws attention to its fundamental nature as a series of choices between alternative

---

[1] As we shall see, certain conventions of valuation are adopted.
[2] There may, of course, have been better alternatives which were not taken into consideration, either through the incapacity of the management or because of the unacceptably high cost in money, time and trouble of preparing more than a certain number of alternative plans.

conference meetings, and by suitable geographical arrangements of offices, laboratories, etc., designed to bring about similar informal personal relationships.)

At the first formal budget meeting we could expect to find the heads of departments, armed with rough drafts—'first approximations'—of their budgets, sitting under the chairmanship of the general manager to consider how far these drafts accorded with the intentions of the board of directors, as interpreted by the general manager, and to discuss the implications of each budget for the other budgets. From one or more such meetings, during which changes would be made in the original drafts, we might expect agreement to be reached within limits sufficiently narrow to allow each head of department to go ahead with the preparation of a more detailed plan, knowing that he would not be wasting time and resources on the preparations of plans wholly inconsistent with those of his colleagues.

Just how exact these plans are will vary greatly. In some businesses—e.g. those selling goods subject to annual changes of fashion—it may be necessary at the early budget meetings to come to definite decisions about what is to be sold next year. The design of the goods may have to be settled in some detail. A decision of this kind may obviously require very close co-operation and consultation between departments at all stages. In other businesses—for example jobbing engineering contractors—it may be impossible to make more than a very rough forecast of the kind of work to be expected. A road transport business evidently has different kinds of budgeting problems from a furniture manufacturer, and so on. Usually it will be possible to plan certain aspects of the business in greater detail than others. These parts will vary with different businesses, as the reader can easily verify by thinking about some of the different kinds of business with which his daily life brings him into contact.

After the preliminary meeting or meetings it is for each department to prepare its detailed budget. The sales manager now knows in greater or less detail the kind and amount of products he will be expected to sell next year. He must now express this selling plan in numerical form. Estimates must be made of quantities of each product to be sold at given prices, and in given localities, month by month, perhaps even week by week, and of changes in the stocks to be held. These numerical forecasts will be agreed with the production department to ensure that the respective budgets are consistent in terms of physical quantities. From them will be calculated the figures of planned sales revenue. Closely interrelated with them will be the budget of the selling expenses (e.g. advertising). The sales revenue figures must also be checked for consistency with the estimates of changes in debtors on which depend the estimates of cash inflows. Each other department of the business will have to go through the same kind of procedure.

The final stage will be reached when each department has a detailed budget which is a numerical value statement of its plan for next year's work that has been found consistent with the budget of each other department, and when all the budgets together have been approved by the general manager and the board of directors.

The choices that determine the figures that appear in the budgets are likely to be made in the first instance by the various departmental heads. It will be necessary, however, for the actual putting together of the figures to be placed in a single pair of hands. Unless one person is given this responsibility it is likely that inconsistencies will develop between the budgets of different departments. Co-ordination is necessary. Furthermore, the translation of physical business activities into money value terms is in some degree a skilled process requiring special training and experience. The person responsible for the budget co-ordination must, if he is to do his job well, not only be alive to the economic implications of given actions, some of them perhaps quite remote, but he must have the technical ability to build up his budgets in a form that will lend itself readily to the subsequent process of control by comparison of budgets with actual results. This is largely a matter of handling large—sometimes very large—masses of numerical data which must be analysed in many ways.

For these reasons the chief executive responsible for the budget preparation is usually a man trained in accounting. Usually he will be responsible also for the accounting work of the business: the recording of what has happened as well as what is planned. In our hypothetical business we have called him the controller, but his title varies: he might be called the chief accountant in another business. In a business of any size some of his subordinates will be concerned with budgeting and others with accounting. He is also likely to be the executive responsible for the financial aspects of the business—the raising of new capital and the investing of funds that are in excess of current business needs. This is a separate function from the co-ordinating work of budgeting and accounting and could, indeed, be in the hands of a separate finance executive. In practice it is often convenient, however, to make the budget co-ordinator and accountant also responsible for finance, because his specialized training fits him particularly well for this work.

We can recapitulate by saying that there must be (a) arithmetical, and (b) technical and economic, consistency in the budgets. The sales figure in the sales revenue budget must, for example, tie in with the figure in the finance budget representing the cash that will be received from debtors as the result of the sales.[1] This arithmetical consistency is essentially an accounting problem and as such is the direct responsibility of the person who performs the function of controller.

On the technical and economic side, it is no good preparing a sales budget that requires, e.g. the sale of 100,000 units, if the business plans do not provide for these to be available for sale from current production, existing stocks, or purchases from outside suppliers, or a combination of these three. The production plan in turn is dependent upon the physical equipment and the manpower which it is planned to make available; and so on. Again, the sales values budgeted must be based upon a given quantity to be sold at a given price. If the market conditions are not consistent with the sale of this quantity at this price there is a fundamental defect in the budget.

The job of ensuring that there is technical and economic consistency is that of the departmental managers and ultimately of the general management (no doubt advised by a budget committee drawn from the various departments, on which the controller or his representative will sit) and of the board of directors. A good controller can be of great value here, however, for while he is normally not a specialist in any of the operating departments of the business,

[1] The calculation will of course allow for possible bad debts, and so on; but the calculation must start from the budgeted sales figure.

B

he will, if he is worth his salt, have a good general knowledge of the business and be able, not only to help the departmental heads in making their figures arithmetically consistent with those of their colleagues, but also to detect technical and economic inconsistencies.

Business budgets are usually thought of as plans expressed in money values. It follows from what we have written, however, that it is possible at least to conceive of the budgeting process as covering every aspect of the business, and including a detailed plan for the behaviour of every employee and every piece of equipment for every hour of the period budgeted for. It would be necessary to ensure that all these plans, including the money value budgets, were, so far as could be seen, mutually consistent. In practice of course such detailed planning would not be possible. Nevertheless, the picture is not without illustrative value. Indeed, in a carefully run business there will be, in addition to the money value budgets, a good many detailed written plans, whether called budgets or not, of the physical activities.

For example, behind the sales revenue budget will stand a budget the figures in which represent the quantities of the various products to be sold; and there will be plans expressing the number of salesmen that will be employed and what they will do, plans for distributing the products, and so on. Behind the production cost budgets will stand the budgets or plans of physical amounts to be produced, of capital equipment available, of labour, of materials to be used, of the times required for various jobs, and so on.

We are now ready to examine the organization of the budgeting and accounting data in our business. Our study must begin from a defined situation however. The next chapter will accordingly introduce the form of accounting statement known as a balance sheet. The function of this is to provide a description of the economic position of a person or organization at a given moment of time. We shall let our starting point be the beginning of one of our company's accounting years.

3

THE BALANCE SHEET

AT ANY given moment of time any business has a certain endowment of economic resources and is subject to certain financial obligations. The accountant's way of summarizing these is to prepare a balance sheet. This document in its conventional form is divided into two main sections in which are classified:

(a) The recorded values of the business's resources. These are the 'assets'.

(b) The claims against the assets. These are sub-divided into:

(i) The recorded amounts of financial obligations of the business to organizations and people *other* than the owners. These non-ownership claims on the business are the 'liabilities'.

(ii) The arithmetical difference between the sum of (a) and the sum of (b) (i). This is the recorded net value of the business from the point of view of its owners: the claim of the owners on the business. (It is sometimes called the 'net worth'.) In a company the owners are the shareholders[1] and this claim is sub-classified in such a way as to indicate how the various parts of it first arose, and to distinguish between different classes of shareholders, i.e. between classes of owners with different legal rights.

Table 3.1 contains the balance sheet of our company on January 1, 19—. It is in the standard traditional form, modified and simplified in certain respects.

---

[1] The strict legal position is that the shareholders own the company, a fictitious person, and the company owns the business.

35

TABLE 3.1

BALANCE SHEET—JANUARY 1 19—

CLAIMS	£	£
Non-ownership Claims = Liabilities		
Long and Medium Term Liabilities:		
Debenture carrying interest at 4% p.a. ..	15,000	
Future income tax on last year's profit, payable in one year's time	8,000	
Current Liabilities:		
Trade creditors 14,000		
Income tax on the profits of the year before last, and profits tax on last year's profit 8,100		
Dividends to be paid to shareholders .. 1,650	23,750	
Total Liabilities		46,750
Shareholders' Claims = Difference between Total Assets and Total Liabilities		
Ordinary Shareholders:		
Capital paid in	12,000	
Profits earned and not distributed ..	81,114	
		93,114
Preference Shareholders:		
Capital paid in carrying a cumulative dividend of 5% p.a.	10,000	
Total Shareholders' Claims (Net Worth) ..		103,114
Total Claims		149,864

ASSETS	£	£
Fixed Assets:		
Land and buildings	27,500	
Plant, machinery and equipment ..	31,500	
		59,000
Current Assets:		
Stocks:		
Raw materials 8,245		
Work-in-progress 12,410		
Finished goods 12,449		
	33,104	
Trade debtors	35,760	
Investments	5,000	
Cash at bank	17,000	
		90,864
Total Assets		149,864

This balance sheet is not drafted for legal purposes under the Companies Act.

On the right-hand side is a list of the assets and their recorded values. These add up to £149,864. On the left-hand side, in the top section, is a list of the liabilities, totalling £46,750. In the lower section are the shareholders' claims, sub-divided according to the way in which different parts arose, and by classes of shareholders. The total of the shareholders' claims is by definition equal to the difference between the assets and the liabilities: £103,114. The right-hand side shows the assets, the left-hand side the claims against these assets.[1]

The general significance of the items in this balance sheet is not difficult to understand. We consider first the assets. The company owns land and buildings and plant, machinery and other equipment, needed for its operations. It possesses stocks of raw materials that will be used in the manufacture of its products. There are partly-finished goods in the process of manufacture (work-in-progress) and finished manufactured goods. The company is owed money by some of its customers—trade debtors. It has some investments and some money in the bank.

The assets, following a well-established convention, are divided into two main groups, 'fixed' and 'current'. Fixed assets are those that form part of the more or less permanent and less liquid equipment of the business: the part that can be less easily or less conveniently converted quickly into money. Current assets are the others. The assets as a whole are arranged in approximate order of increasing liquidity.

We now turn to the claims. The company has borrowed money at interest over and above the amounts provided by its shareholders. This is the debenture. It also owes money to the tax authorities and expects to owe more in future. There are debts due to people—trade creditors—who have recently supplied it with materials. It is soon going to pay its own shareholders a dividend and this is regarded as a debt owing by the company, no longer part of the more permanent shareholders' claims.

---

[1] It is the usual British convention to list assets on the right-hand side and claims on the left-hand side. This is however quite arbitrary and the opposite convention is followed in the U.S.A. Sometimes liabilities are deducted from assets in a single column and the difference explained in a lower section summarizing the shareholders' claims. Other arrangements are possible.

The liabilities are divided into (a) long and medium term and (b) current liabilities. This division corresponds broadly to the fixed asset and current asset categories on the assets side of the balance sheet. The current liabilities are obligations of the company that will be settled within a relatively short period. The longer term obligations are the remainder.

The rough test of whether a figure is classified as a fixed or a current asset, or as a long and medium term liability or a current liability, is the period between its acquisition and the date when it will (if an asset) be turned into cash or (if a liability) be settled by a cash payment. If this period is less than one year it may be said, as a rough approximation, that the accountant's classification will be 'current'. The rule is, however, only a rough one and there are exceptions and border-line cases.[1]

The section of the balance sheet that summarizes the claims of the shareholders shows that the net business resources, taken together, owe their origin to:

(a) money paid in by the 'ordinary' shareholders;[2]

(b) money paid in by the 'preference' shareholders;[2]

(c) the profit (so far as this has not been distributed or is about to be distributed).

The legal rights of shareholders of different classes vary, but the usual arrangement is that the preference shareholders provide money to the company on the understanding that any profit earned shall first be used in paying them a fixed annual dividend—in Table 3.1, 5 per cent of the amount paid in—in priority to the ordinary shareholders, and that should the company come to an end ('liquidate' or 'wind-up' as it is called) they shall receive, out of whatever surplus resources remain when all the liabilities have been paid, and before the ordinary shareholders receive anything, a fixed amount equal to the amount they originally paid in (or frequently

---

[1] For example, the stock of raw materials for manufacturing purposes will be classified as current even if it is intended to hold part of it for several years.

[2] 'Money' here includes 'money's worth': value may be contributed in other forms than cash.

quantities to be sold into the revenue to be received must be in accordance with expected market conditions. It must be consistent with the production cost budgets in that these must reflect the cost of producing the relevant quantity of goods after allowing for expected changes in the stocks of finished goods. It does not always follow, however, that a close estimate of the quantities of different kinds of goods to be sold can be made. The nature of the business may be such that exactly what is to be sold cannot be determined in advance, though past experience indicates that a certain aggregate sales value is likely to be attained. In Chapter 5 we shall indicate how production requirements can be related to such an estimate.

TABLE 4.2

SALES QUANTITY BUDGET 19—

Units of Product

	Jan.–Mar.	April–June	July–Sept.	Oct.–Dec.	Year
Type A	27,000	40,500	55,000	27,500	150,000
Type B	63,000	44,000	39,000	54,000	200,000

Sales revenue control

The budget states the planned revenue; the accounts record, day by day, the actual revenue. The figures of the latter are classified and accumulated in a form that corresponds with the budget, so that the results can be compared conveniently with the plans. The sales revenue of our business will be recorded and analysed into sales of type A and of type B, quarter by quarter. The periodic totals will be incorporated into reports for the sales manager. All this is part of the work of the controller's department. The kind of report one would expect to find is shown in Table 4.3.

TABLE 4.3

SALES—MARCH QUARTER 19—

£

		Budget	Actual	Variance*
Type A	..	54,000	53,614	— 386
Type B	..	31,500	33,001	+ 1,501
Total	..	85,500	86,615	+ 1,115

* Adverse variances are shown as negative amounts.

A report of this type can be likened to the comparison a navigator makes between his astronomical observations and his previously plotted course. The word 'variance', which heads the third column of figures, is here used for the difference, positive or negative, between the budgeted figure and the actual figure. (It is convenient to call an adverse variance—here a shortfall of sales revenue— negative, and a favourable one positive.) In general, the management will be more interested in the variance column of the report than in the other columns, since the variances indicate deviations from a plan that is already known. The study of variances is sometimes called 'control by difference'.

If the variances are sufficiently large to be thought significant, the next step is to investigate their causes. These fall into two main classes. First, the investigation may show that the original estimates were either bad ones or that, though they were sound in the light of the information originally available, they became incorrect owing to conditions that could not have been foreseen. In either case it may be necessary to revise the budgets for the remainder of the year. (This may mean revising not only the budget on which the variance appears, but some or all of the other budgets. In practice it is usually convenient to revise, not by altering the original budget figures— which will by now be fixed in the minds of all concerned—but by calculating the future variances now expected from the original figures.) In either case, too, the lesson learnt may be relevant when next year's budgets are prepared.

Secondly, the general management may think, rightly or wrongly, that the original budgets are still valid. In this case the variance is, by definition, attributable to mistakes in carrying out the business plan. The sales manager may be asked to improve his organization; possibly, particularly if the trouble persists, it may be decided that changes must be made in the staff of the sales department. Care is necessary however. Perhaps the failure was due, not to mistakes in the sales department, but to errors elsewhere. Perhaps the production department has been turning out defective goods, the rejection of which by customers has brought down the sales figures. As always, the interdependence of the different parts of the business must not be forgotten. (It may be argued that if the production department was at fault the original sales budgets were no longer

The two figures, £2,300 and £1,900, are statistical indicators. By valuing the adverse quantity variance at the budgeted price we show the effect on profit *if* the smaller quantity had been sold at the budgeted price. By applying the favourable price variance to the sales actually made we obtain an indicator of the effect the price change would have had *if* it had occurred without changing the quantity sold. The figures thus obtained are, it must be emphasized, merely a convenient way of bringing to the attention of the reader the results of the market situation: *by themselves they have no absolute significance*. They may, for example, reflect the fact that a particular market for some 1,150 units closed up completely while in other markets conditions were favourable for a higher price. They may reflect the degree of what is called the elasticity of demand in a given market, indicating that the loss in sales, caused by a rise in price, was not fully balanced by the higher revenue from the sales made. They may merely reflect errors in forecasting the price-quantity relationships. Their primary function is to start the user thinking along certain lines.

It is most important to appreciate that there are many occasions in accounting where an attempt to be too precise or too accurate is a waste of time, money and effort. The most any of the above figures can do is to *suggest* to the management that here are certain matters that might well be investigated. No method of analysis can be said to be more 'correct' or 'accurate' than another. That method is best which most helps the management. Many people would have been satisfied with the simple statements of Tables 4.3 and 4.4. Others like more elaborate calculations (though we suspect it is often the accountants rather than the managers who favour the elaboration). This argument applies to most accounting figures when they are used as economic indicators—i.e. as guides to decisions. We are not suggesting that when one wants to know the amount of money at the bank more than one answer can be satisfactory: this is a simple counting problem which has only one right answer, though even here for *some* purposes an approximation correct to, say, the nearest £1,000 will suffice. The amount of accuracy needed in accounting varies in fact with the situation, as any sensible accountant knows.

In setting out the above examples we have been illustrating a very simple application of what is called 'standard costing'. ('Costing' is not, as the name seems to imply, restricted to the study of cost in a narrow sense. It is equally concerned with the study of revenue and profits and losses.) Standard costing can perhaps most usefully be described as the application of methods of planning and control by budgets to particular business operations as distinct from the business as a whole. There is, however, no clear-cut line between planning and control by budgets and by standard costing. The essence of both is the careful estimation, before the event, of the economic results of a particular business operation or set of operations, the subsequent comparison of actual results with the estimates, and the study and analysis of the results of this comparison in various ways.

The accounting system

The physical aspect of sales accounting begins with the customer's order. As the orders come in, each is recorded and given a serial number so that it can be identified later and cross-referenced. If machine or electronic accounting is in use this number may be needed as a code allowing the machine to identify the order. All later documents or records relating to this order can be connected with it by this number.

One of the functions of the orders record is to maintain control over the fulfilment of orders. It will, therefore, be someone's job to watch the record and make sure that orders are not neglected. The orders record also provides a check on outgoing goods. Each delivery is matched by an order. This reduces the risk of fraudulent despatch of goods to consignees who are not bona-fide customers.

When an order is received the section concerned with the despatch of goods is informed by the sales department where the goods are to go, and of any special instructions to be observed with respect to packing and method of conveyance. When the goods are sent out a delivery note goes with them to tell the customer what he is receiving. This is cross-referenced to enable him to identify it with his original order. At the same time the department that releases the goods advises the accounting and the sales departments so that both know what action has been taken at any particular time with respect to a given order.

When the accounting department knows that the goods have gone, it sends to the customer the invoice or bill—the formal notice of his newly-incurred debt for the goods. The business now has a new asset—the debt, and the owners—the shareholders—have enjoyed an increase in their claim on the business. At the same time the business has relinquished another asset—the goods despatched—and the shareholders' claim is simultaneously reduced by the value of these.

These balance sheet changes are recorded in the formal double-entry records. We consider first the sale. An increase in the class of assets 'trade debtors' (see Table 3.1) is recorded. This is traditionally described as a 'debit' in the accounts, that is, as the entry of a positive quantity in the accounting system. Corresponding to this debit a 'credit' is recorded in the form of an increase in the 'sales revenue'. This is really part of the profit section of the shareholders' claim (see Table 3.1) but is classified separately, as in any particular period it is necessary to analyse the profit by cause. As this entry records an increase in claims on the business it is a credit or negative quantity.

We now consider the despatch of the goods. This calls for a reduction in the asset 'finished goods' (see Table 3.1). There is a corresponding reduction in the profit section of the shareholders' claim (the business no longer has to account to its owners for the value of these goods) and this is made under the sub-classification 'cost of sales'. The reduction in finished goods reduces an asset, i.e. it reduces a debit or positive amount, and is therefore itself a credit or negative entry. The reduction in profit on the other hand reduces a claim, i.e. it reduces a credit or negative amount, and is itself therefore a debit or positive entry.

The decrease in the finished goods will, under the normal accounting conventions, usually be a smaller amount than the increase in the debtors, for the finished goods will be valued on the basis of the cost of the goods without the addition of profit, whereas the debt includes profit. Hence there will be, as the result of the sale, a net increase in the recorded value of assets and a similar net increase in the shareholders' claim. The latter is a component of the net profit or loss for the year.

As already noted, it is convenient for analytical purposes to separate the recording of the sale—the increase in debtors and its cause—from the recording of the reduction in finished goods held. The latter has been mentioned here for the sake of clarity. Its relation to the budgeting system will, however, be considered in a later chapter.

If any readers are confused by the fact that a component of profit is given a negative sign in the double-entry system they should remind themselves that the earning of profit is tantamount to an increase in the net assets of the company (i.e. net of any increase in claims of outside creditors). If a profit is earned the company has henceforth more to account for to its shareholders—it 'owes' them more. As the accounts all reflect the *company's point of view* there is an increase in claims equal to the increase in net assets, and this is negative. It is, however, essential to distinguish between claims of shareholders and claims of outside creditors. This is achieved in practice by an appropriate nomenclature.

The accounting system thus reflects the balance sheet pattern by maintaining at all times an equality between assets and claims, the former being regarded as positive (or debits) and the latter as negative (or credits). The double-entry system is therefore (apart from errors) always in balance: the algebraic sum of all the amounts recorded is zero. The analysis of the changes in the shareholders' claim enables us to identify the particular revenues and costs which explain these changes. (Changes due to additional funds paid into or withdrawn from the business by the shareholders are, of course, classified separately.)

The figures of each accounting classification are summarized in a statistical table called an 'account'. In the traditional form of double-entry, whether a number is positive or negative is indicated by its position in the account, left-hand numbers being debits (positive) and right-hand numbers credits (negative)—except in the traditional English balance sheet, as shown in Table 3.1, in which this convention is, for historical reasons, reversed. As machine accounting develops, however, whether an item is a debit or a credit will increasingly be indicated by other forms of coding.

The essential function of this formal accounting system is to maintain effective control over the data by establishing orderly and systematic procedures, including the maintenance of continuous checks on the arithmetical consistency of the different classifications. In other words, the double-entry system provides a controlled set of basic records. The data in these can be subjected to further analysis at will and is used as the basis of the periodic accounting reports for the management, the shareholders and the income tax authorities.

One of the most characteristic features of the double-entry system is the maintenance of accounts corresponding to given responsibilities. Thus, the account that records the value of finished goods reflects the responsibility of the storekeeper to produce, if called upon to do so, goods of equivalent amount to the balance shown on the account—the opening stock recorded *plus* additions *minus* deductions. When goods are despatched this balance is reduced to correspond to the fall in the storekeeper's responsibility. At the same time the balance of the trade debtors account is increased to reflect the simultaneous rise in the responsibility of the section of the accounting department that is responsible for debt collection. The shareholders' claims, taken in aggregate, reflect the responsibility of the board of directors to the shareholders.

It may happen that goods sent to customers are, for one reason or another, rejected or returned, or that a reduction is made in the original charge. The accounting arrangements for this are essentially similar to those already described for sales transactions except that the entries in the records are of opposite sign. The record of the reduction in the sales revenue corresponding to the drop in the customer's debt is maintained under a separate classification, since knowledge of the numerical value of these 'returns' and 'allowances' is of importance to the management: a substantial rise in the figure may indicate increasing inefficiency.

Accounting entries that record reductions in assets will receive particular attention. For example, the debtors' accounts are usually the main evidence of the debts and are the main control over the debt collection procedure. An erroneous or fraudulent reduction in the debts recorded may cause loss to the business just as much as would the theft of cash from the safe. (The fraud might take, for example, the form of an agreement with a customer to cancel his debt in the accounts; or a customer might pay and an employee might steal the money before it reached the accounts, then cancelling the debt record to prevent the customer from being asked for payment a second time.) The accounting procedure will reduce this risk by arranging for any reduction in the debts to be recorded independently of the corresponding reduction in sales revenue or rise in cash, and by a different person. If a credit is recorded in one account without a corresponding debit in another an arithmetical difference will become apparent when the totals are summed, as they will be at frequent, perhaps daily, intervals, and this will invite investigation. Compensating errors may occur and if fraud is involved there may be collusion, but at least the number of possible mishaps is reduced.

This still leaves the risk that the original initiating data that reaches the accounting staff may be incorrect. In the case of the sales records the main accounting problem is that of ensuring that the proper debt record is created when the goods leave the premises: hence the arrangements that are made for notification of despatch and for a check on the fulfilment of orders. In the case of returns or allowances, however, the problem is that of making certain the reduction in the debt record is matched, either by an approved return of goods, or by a specific authority to make the customer an allowance. This requires a procedure for special authorization of reductions in debt when the goods are returned or when no goods are returned but there is still to be an allowance to the customer.

All these arrangements form part of the system of internal accounting control.[1] The formulation of such a system, embracing the flow of information, the allocation of duties, and systematic accounting, is an interesting exercise in applied logic, requiring an analytical approach, a knowledge of the technical possibilities of accounting and documentation, and an appreciation of the nature of the particular business which is being studied.

We have not considered the various means which can be used to record and classify the flow of information. These range from a simple counting house organization of people, paper, pens and ink, to a data-processing system centred on an electronic digital computer. Some degree of mechanization is now found in most offices. Most of the larger ones are highly mechanized, using keyboard

---

[1] To be distinguished from 'budgetary control', the continuing control over the fulfilment of the economic plans of the business.

accounting machines or punched cards. As electronic computers become cheaper and their capacities better known and understood this process will no doubt be carried further.

This concludes our survey of the accounting arrangements with respect to sales.

Our discussion of sales accounting arrangements has given us the opportunity to refer to the general principles of double-entry accounting. We shall devote less attention to this in the later chapters.

We now turn to production.

5

PRODUCTION—I

The production plans

The production plans are concerned with the work to be done, quarter by quarter, in each department of the factory. We start by considering the planning of the quantities of finished goods that are wanted. These are calculated in the finished goods quantity budget (Table 5.1).

The first row of figures in this table for each type of goods corresponds with the set of budgeted sales figures in Table 4.2. These are the quantities that are planned to be sold. To these are added the quantities of finished goods that are planned to be in stock at the end of each quarter. From the resultant totals are deducted the stocks at the beginning of each quarter. The remainders, shown in the final row, are the quantities to be produced (or bought from another business) if the plan is to be fulfilled.

TABLE 5.1

FINISHED GOODS QUANTITY BUDGET 19—

Units of Product

	Jan.– March	April– June	July– Sept.	Oct.– Dec.	Year
Type A:					
Sales (table 4.2)	27,000	40,500	55,000	27,500	150,000
Closing stock	16,500	22,500	1,500	3,000	3,000
	43,500	63,000	56,500	30,500	153,000
Opening stock	3,000	16,500	22,500	1,500	3,000
Production	40,500	46,500	34,000	29,000	150,000

materials cost budget, as shown in Table 5.2. Behind this money value budget there lies an implied materials quantity budget of considerable complexity covering a great number of different supplies. The theoretical procedure is simple: you plan the work to be done during each period, calculate the quantity of each material implied by that work, price the quantities, and sum the results. This demands close liaison between the purchasing staff

TABLE 5.2

PRODUCTION MATERIALS COST BUDGET 19—

£

	Jan.–March	April–June	July–Sept.	Oct.–Dec.	Year
Direct materials:					
Type A	39,900	43,225	30,637	28,738	142,500
Type B	8,137	7,175	8,313	11,025	34,650
Indirect materials	2,613	2,648	2,451	2,488	10,200
Total ..	50,650	53,048	41,401	42,251	187,350

and the production staff. The final decision about the nature of the materials to be used will depend among other things upon technical requirements and upon expected material prices. At a given price it may pay to substitute a material less efficient technically because this is counterbalanced by its relative cheapness; at another price it may be the other way round.

Although the general problem is soon stated, the physical work of compiling such a budget may be very great. Unless fast mechanical, electrical or electronic methods of compiling data are available, or unless the manufacture of each product calls for only a small quantity of materials and there are only a few products, it will probably not be possible to make very precise estimates. Even with modern aids to computation this may not be possible. Some-times—perhaps more often than not—the production materials cost will be calculated by assuming that a given relationship holds between production and material consumption when both are stated in value terms, thus eliminating the problem of estimating consumption in quantity terms for each item of materials for a year in advance. If the sales revenue estimate has not been based on a detailed quantitative estimate of goods to be sold (*see* p. 43) this approach may be inevitable.[1]

Thus it might be assumed that total material cost was on average 40 per cent of the expected sales value of production. Assumptions of this kind seldom turn out to be exact; but they may well be accurate enough for practical purposes—that is, as accurate as is possible with the given staff and equipment of the business, and very likely with any staff or equipment. No economic forecast can be more than a 'best approximation'.

The classification of the material used in production into 'direct' and 'indirect' is an application of the principle of classifying costs as far as possible into groups which are homogeneous with respect to their behaviour, that is, which are likely to vary in the same way in response to a given stimulus. In other words we try to classify in one group expenses for which the laws of change are similar. It is seldom possible to achieve complete homogeneity because to do so would usually mean having so many classifications that the figures would become difficult to handle and would lose a good deal of their significance. The whole problem, indeed, is one of holding a balance between very little classification, which may leave the management with little guidance, and very extensive classification, which may make useful generalization impossible.

Thus, if we assumed as above that the total material cost would be x per cent of total sales value, our material cost budget would consist of a single row of figures obtained by applying x per cent to the budgeted sales value of production (allowing for work only partly finished at the beginning and end of the periods) for each quarter and for the year. In some businesses this might be an acceptable approach because all the materials tended to vary in direct proportion to output, and because all the products required the same kinds of material in similar proportions, or the materials used were all of a similar type and price. Or these conditions might not be fulfilled, but the uncertainties of the business might be so great that a rough approximation of this type, based on previous experience and consideration of the future, was as good a figure as could be obtained. It is likely, however, that more reliable estimates

---

[1] It will still be necessary in the shorter run to plan the physical material requirements as part of the production planning.

by an expected average hourly wage cost rate, which we call a standard wage cost rate. By applying a standard cost rate to any variation in the direct labour time from the expected or standard time, we have an indicator of the order of magnitude of the cost of changes in labour efficiency—i.e. an indicator of the *approximate* effect on the business profit if the variances persist. By applying standard rates to standard output—labour time relationships we also have indicators of the approximate direct labour cost of changes in output within certain limits. If the direct labour force employed is allowed to vary immediately there is a change in activity, these indicators measure changes in actual money outlay more or less precisely. If, as is more likely, there is a substantial lag in the adjustment of the labour force to changes in activity, we still have money value indicators of the longer run effects of changes, which also serve as short run indicators of the value of the labour made available for (or withdrawn from) other activities inside the business.

The usefulness of these indicators does not depend upon their showing the precise amount of immediate gains or losses in money terms—this they often cannot do—but in giving the management an idea of the orders of magnitude involved in favourable or adverse variances from plans, and in decisions.

A knowledge of the direct labour time planned in a given period (and therefore, with given wage rates, of the direct labour cost) may sometimes be useful in forecasting sales revenue: the business may be engaged, for example, in government contracting, the remuneration for which is based on, or can be expressed as a fixed percentage of, direct labour cost.

A refined system of analysis might avoid the rather crude classification of cost into direct and indirect, and express the total labour cost as a function of the output by means of a more complex formula. There is a good deal of scope for developments of this kind based on statistical investigation of the relationships between cost and output. There is no doubt that such refinements are possible in some businesses. In others the uncertainties may continue to require simpler and rougher methods. The examples in this book will be based on the traditional direct and indirect classifications.

The budget figures for direct labour cost are obtained by multiplying the planned hours of direct labour time by the appropriate wage cost rates, making necessary allowances for bonus rates, overtime, etc., required by the production programme, thus arriving at a standard weighted average rate. Sometimes the direct labour cost may be obtained by formula, e.g. as a percentage of the estimated sales value of production, allowing for changes in partly finished work at the beginning and end of the period. Sometimes it may be enough to assume that the factory will be operating for the full normal working hours during the period, so that total direct labour cost can be estimated in one sum on the basis of previous experience, corrected, if a change in wage rates has taken place or is expected, by applying an appropriate index number to the earlier figures.

Indirect labour cost will include the value, at the wage rates assumed, of such part of the direct labour hours as represent idle time—time assumed not to result in output; the balance will be the wage cost of the indirect labour force. This will normally be estimated department by department, each sectional executive putting up his figures to the budget committee on the basis of the planned production for his department, as with the indirect material cost. Extrapolation from previous years will, as usual, play a substantial part in the estimating process.

Production general expense[1]

This term may be used to cover the cost of services such as power, lighting, heating, rent, rates, insurance, and many others that are sufficiently closely related to the physical production and all the ancillary activities to be the responsibility of the production manager (Table 5.4).

Like material and labour cost, general expense can be divided into direct and indirect expense, the former being defined as cost that varies in direct proportion with the level of output. There is usually little general expense in the 'direct' category and, as its treatment raises no new point of principle (as with material and

[1] 'Expense' tends to be used by accountants for cost other than material and labour cost. There is in this context no difference in meaning between 'expense' and 'cost'.

achieved. In short, budgeting and accounting data acceptable for the purpose of the general control of the business will not always be appropriate for other purposes. This question is discussed further in Chapter 7.

The total amount budgeted for the production department under the heads of direct materials cost, direct labour cost and indirect or 'overhead' cost, is obtained by summing the appropriate totals in the budgets of Tables 5.2, 5.3 and 5.4. The result is the budgeted production cost shown in Table 5.5; this is taken as the conventional measure of the value of the planned output.

In the next chapter we shall consider how the budgets are affected by the existence of partly finished work at the beginning and end of each period; the calculation of standard costs; and the derivation of the budgeted cost of sales.

TABLE 5.5

PRODUCTION COST BUDGET 19—

	Jan.–March	April–June	£ July–Sept.	Oct.–Dec.	Year
Direct cost:					
Type A—					
Material (table 5.2)	39,900	43,225	30,637	28,738	142,500
Labour (table 5.3)	14,700	15,925	11,287	10,588	52,500
	54,600	59,150	41,924	39,326	195,000
Type B—					
Material (table 5.2)	8,137	7,175	8,313	11,025	34,650
Labour (table 5.3)	5,812	5,125	5,938	7,875	24,750
	13,949	12,300	14,251	18,900	59,400
Indirect or over-head cost (tables 5.2, 5.3, 5.4) ..	11,816	11,390	10,963	11,433	45,602
Total ..	80,365	82,840	67,138	69,659	300,002

6

PRODUCTION—II

Work-in-progress

At the beginning of any month or quarter there will usually be some unfinished work-in-progress from the previous period, and at the end of the period there will be work-in-progress to be completed in the next period. The work-in-progress at any time is part of the resources available for production in the ensuing period. This can be put in another way by saying that, given the opening work-in-progress, the work done in each period must be sufficient to produce the output of finished goods required *plus* the planned work-in-progress at the end of the period. The production programme must be drafted accordingly.

The work-in-progress adjustments are relevant if the cost of production is being used as an index of the factory capacity. Experience may establish, for example, an approximate arithmetical relationship between given levels of direct labour cost and the absorption of factory capacity, measured in time. (It might be known, for example, that for the type of goods being produced a total direct labour cost of £80,000 a year was, with the present type of labour force and at current wage rates, equivalent to the maximum use of existing available capacity without working overtime.) The budget committee might then estimate the productive capacity required in a given period by converting the sales value of the goods to be produced into a direct labour cost equivalent, on the basis of the average direct labour cost per £1 of sales revenue, instead of relying on a detailed physical production plan. The figure they obtained would not, however, represent the true direct labour cost equivalent of the productive effort required unless account was taken of the direct labour content of changes in work-in-progress. Failure to do this could lead to under or over estimation of the

74

factory capacity—and the labour force—expected to be absorbed by production. The importance of this issue depends, among other things, on the extent to which the level of work-in-progress varies from one year end to another. If the same kind of products are made, and the level of work-in-progress is constant in physical terms, the physical production effort in the year will correspond to the quantity of finished goods required, and work-in-progress can be ignored. This constancy cannot always be assumed.

Even if careful estimates are made of physical production, it is still useful to compare the budgeted cost, based on the planned physical production, with an estimate of the production cost obtained by applying the approximate cost-selling value ratios to the sales value of the production: if there are serious errors in the first calculation, the second may bring them to light. Suppose, for example, that the physical estimates in the production plan, when converted into value, suggested that total direct labour cost would be £160,000. Suppose also that it was believed that direct labour cost represented roughly 40 per cent of the sales value of finished goods, and that the forecast of the latter was £500,000, so that the estimated direct labour cost was 40 per cent of £500,000, or £200,000. There would be a discrepancy of £40,000 to investigate. The investigation might show that the physical production plan had overestimated the capacity or efficiency of the factory, so that unless efficiency was abnormally high, a good deal of overtime, or the purchase of additional equipment and the hire of more labour, or a substantial amount of sub-contracting, none of which was yet allowed for in the various budgets, would be needed. The discrepancy might, however, merely mean that the level of work-in-progress would be run down by an amount representing a direct labour cost of about £40,000 during the period. Or the investigation might show that the 40 per cent was an overestimate of the direct labour cost content, perhaps because of changes in the character of the products. This, too, would be useful information, for it would indicate that the figures in use for such important procedures as the quotation of prices, or the assessment of the effect on production of taking additional orders, had not been kept up to date.

This operation of checking one set of figures against another is (or should be) continually going on in the controller's department, and is typical of the way in which budget forecasts and accounting data are controlled.

The level of work-in-progress at various dates is also of relevance with respect to the estimation of the profit and the flow of cash. It is necessary to set a value on changes in work-in-progress in order to arrive at the cost of the finished goods, which in turn is needed to determine the cost of the goods sold; profit is an important managerial indicator, and the effect of the work-in-progress valuation has, therefore, to be clear when the profit figure, planned or realized, is studied. The level of work-in-progress affects the amount of cash 'locked up' in the business—money spent and not yet recouped. Other things being equal, more work-in-progress means less cash available for other purposes.

The level and valuation of goods finished, but unsold, are relevant in the profit and finance planning for exactly the same reasons.

We have now reached the point at which it is necessary to turn to the calculation of cost per unit of output before continuing with our study of the budgeting and accounting procedure. There are various ways of dealing with this problem. That of standard costing seems most convenient and useful.

Standard costs
When the budget estimates of material and labour cost, and of general expense, are prepared, assumptions have to be made about the prices of materials and services, and the wage rates, that will prevail. In practice it is convenient to assume some fixity of prices and wages during the budgeting period. If a fairly steady rise (or fall) in prices or wages is in fact expected, average figures may be used in the calculations, it being understood that in the earlier part of the year actual costs may be rather below (or above) the budgeted level and that in the later part of the year this situation may be reversed. (An attempt may even be made to calculate the expected differences month by month and record the effect of these in the budget as 'expected variances'.) Such prices and wage rates are the 'standard prices' and 'standard wage rates'.

The physical aspects of production—the quantities and kinds of materials and components used for particular jobs, the hours of particular kinds of labour required, the hours of use of capital equipment—can be formulated like the prices and wage rates. For each particular operation in the factory it is possible to imagine a detailed description of the physical activities. This description consists of the material specification and the operational plan, whether it be for the making of a particular part for a finished product, the making of the whole product (in which case the making of each part and the assembly of all the parts would be included), or the operation of a whole service department, such as the provision of power.

In every case the general idea behind the use of standards is the application of forethought and the careful description of what is to be done in physical and value terms. What is really being done is to establish *formulae* for particular operations.

Once the standards have been calculated and agreed—'set' as it is called—it is possible to calculate the standard cost of any particular operation. This is merely a matter of multiplying the quantities of materials used, or the times consumed, by the appropriate standard prices or wage rates. The fact that the actual business results will very seldom turn out exactly as forecast is not a relevant criticism of the use of standards, which provide that most important thing, a basis for comparison; the standard price of a particular raw material, for example, can be regarded as an origin from which positive or negative deviations (variances) can be measured. When these variances are studied they are interpreted in the light of the original assumptions upon which the standards were set. (This is an important point: the interpretation of figures must never be divorced from the study of the way they were prepared.) The user of the budgets knows, for example, that a price variance from standard may be merely a statistical difference, due to the use, in setting the standards, of an average of expected actual figures. But he will also be on the look-out for variances greater than those that might reasonably be expected.

The main uses of standard costs are in: (*a*) the construction of the budgets: this becomes much simpler if, once operational production decisions have been made, the physical and value budgets can be built up by putting together the sets of standard figures that correspond to the operations that these decisions comprise; (*b*) deciding what prices to fix and what to produce: such decisions are likely to be more easily made if formulae exist by which an output of a given product can be converted into physical operations and values (the conversion of a given output to value terms by the application of standard costs is not, it should be emphasized, the final step in pricing: prices cannot be fixed regardless of market conditions; but it is important to know the relation between production cost and the price it is hoped to realize); (c) controlling the business operations: control is not likely to be as effective as it might be unless it is possible to relate actual results to some kind of standard; (d) providing convenient working bases for the valuation of stocks of raw materials, work-in-progress and finished goods.

The setting of standards is likely to be quite a complicated matter in practice. It requires a good knowledge of all sides of the business. It is not an accounting job alone, and cannot be done without the co-operation of the technical staff. It is not possible to study the process in detail here, but we shall illustrate the principles by considering how the standard cost of 100 units of type A product might be calculated in our business.

Standard direct material cost
We start with the direct material specification. (Indirect materials will be estimated and accounted for as part of the indirect, or overhead, cost, discussed below.) We shall assume that the specification provides for given quantities of three different direct materials. Let these be X, Y and Z. A standard price per unit for each of these must be set. This will normally be based on the expected current material prices for the period, since it is these that measure the business sacrifice from using the material. With this information we can calculate the standard direct material cost of 100 units of type A (Table 6.1).

Standard direct labour cost
The direct labour cost is usually calculated with respect to what are called 'cost centres'. A cost centre is really a name for a particular operation, or a group of operations of a similar type, for which a given person is responsible. A given product will require the service of specified cost centres. Thus one cost centre might be that for machining raw material by grinding; another might

TABLE 6.1

DIRECT MATERIAL COST 19—

Type A 100 units

Material	Quantity lb.	Standards Price per lb. £	Cost £
X	30	1·55	46·5
Y	2	15·70	31·4
Z	5	3·42	17·1
Total			95·0

be for a different type of machining, for example, milling; a third might be polishing. The operational layout for a particular product specifies each operation, showing what is to be done, where it is to be done, and how long it should take. By estimating the labour cost per hour at each centre we obtain a standard hourly rate. By applying this standard hourly rate to the time specified for performing the operation on a given quantity of a particular product we arrive at the standard cost of that operation on that product. By adding together the standard costs for all operations we obtain the aggregate direct labour cost for a given quantity of final output.

This method of building up the standard cost by cost centres facilitates the calculation of a standard cost for a new product, or the revision of the standard cost of an existing product, once the appropriate manufacturing operations for the product have been specified. It also facilitates control, because variances between actual cost and standard cost can be studied by particular cost centres, an essential requirement if action is to be taken to improve performance and cost estimating.

Most industrial processes involve a large number of operations. Calculating the labour cost of producing a given product is rather like putting together a jig-saw puzzle. The cost centre is a device for dividing the puzzle into manageable sections. In practice the calculation proceeds in two steps. If we are considering a particular product we ascertain the standard direct labour cost for each cost centre concerned. From these figures we can build up a departmental direct labour cost by aggregating the cost for the various cost centres that will be used for the product in each works department.[1] Aggregating the departmental costs gives us the factory, or works, direct labour cost of a given quantity of the product.

Apart from making the calculations more manageable, this process has the advantage of giving us the standard cost by areas of subordinate responsibility. We have already noted the advantage of classifying variances by cost centres; the same argument applies to departments, though here we are watching the results of departmental managers instead, as in the case of the cost centres, of the foremen or charge hands. If a given department has a continual record of adverse variances this will probably tell us something about its manager.

For the sake of simplicity we shall assume that the works departments concerned with making type A contain only one cost centre per department. In other words, the calculation to be shown will be that relevant to a cost centre, but it will refer to the whole works department, which in this case, therefore, will itself be a cost centre. (This will save us the arithmetical work of aggregating the figures of a number of cost centres in order to obtain the departmental cost.) We shall assume that the operations are carried out in three such works departments, numbered 1, 2 and 3. The aggregation of the figures for these departments gives us the total standard direct labour cost for the product (Table 6.2).

TABLE 6.2

DIRECT LABOUR COST 19—

Type A 100 units

Cost Centre				Time	Standards Rate	Cost
				hours	£	£
1 ..	..	..	..	14·7	·231	3·4
2 ..	..	..	..	120·0	·172	20·6
3 ..	..	..	..	58·5	·188	11·0
Total	..	..	..	..	..	35·0

[1] These works departments are sub-departments of the production department as a whole and are all under the control of the production manager.

a kind of loss due to the failure to keep the plant normally occupied.[1] 'Normal' cannot be given a precise significance in general; it must be consciously assessed for each case and the figures interpreted in the light of the assessment.

The allocation of overhead cost to a cost centre involves arbitrary decisions. Such an allocation is based on two main principles. The first is that, in general, all the expected production cost should be allocated to the various cost centres. The second is that the allocation should give as good an index as possible of the sacrifice involved in using a given cost centre—as compared with not using it—in the longer run. For reasons that will be discussed later, 'as good as possible' may in fact be very poor. Nor can a precise meaning be attached to the 'longer run'. Because no clear-cut criteria are involved there may well be differences of opinion as to the best bases of allocation. The general idea, however, is that if one cost centre involves the use of more expensive space and equipment, etc. than another, the hourly rate of the former should, other things being equal, be higher.

The allocation of cost to cost centres requires, then, the following steps:

(a) All overhead cost that would be saved if a cost centre did not exist is allocated to that cost centre. This would include, for example, depreciation of the equipment of the cost centre.

(b) All cost that would be saved if a works department did not exist (other than that already allocated under (a)) is allocated to that department.

(c) The cost of works service departments is allocated to production departments on a proportionate basis that as far as possible reflects the relative use made by each of its services.

(d) The cost allocated to each production department under (b) and (c) is spread among cost centres in that department on the same basis as in (c), e.g. the departmental rent may be allocated to cost centres in proportion to the space each occupies.

[1] From a balance sheet point of view the production cost represented by this variance represents a fall in the ownership claim, instead of the creation of work-in-progress or finished goods.

The hourly cost rate for each centre multiplied by the normal budgeted hours available at that cost centre, summed across all cost centres, equals the total budgeted production overhead cost.

The calculation of the standard overhead hourly rates for the production of type A gives, we will assume, the figures shown in the rate column of Table 6.3. The time column contains the same standard times as those that appeared in Table 6.2. From these two columns we obtain, by multiplication, in the cost column, the standard overhead production cost per 100 units.

TABLE 6.3

OVERHEAD COST 19—

Type A 100 units

				Standards		
Cost Centre				Time	Rate	Cost
				hours	£	£
1 ..	..	..	..	14·7	·340	5·0
2 ..	..	..	..	120·0	·123	14·8
3 ..	..	..	..	58·5	·051	3·0
Total	..	..	..	..	..	22·8

We can now combine Tables 6.1., 6.2 and 6.3 and obtain a total standard cost per 100 units for type A. This sums, as Table 6.4 shows, to £152.8 or £1. 10s. 7d. per unit produced.

TABLE 6.4

STANDARD COST STATEMENT 19—

Type A 100 units

						£
Standard direct material cost (Table 6.1)	..		..			95·0
Standard direct labour cost (Table 6.2)	..		..			35·0
Standard overhead cost (Table 6.3)		..		..		22·8
Total	..	..	..	..	..	152·8
Standard unit cost	..	..	..	..	..	£1. 10s. 7d.

We shall discuss later how these standard costs may be used for control purposes. Meanwhile we return to the valuation of work-in-progress and finished goods.

We value each piece of partly or wholly finished product by summing the standard costs for the processes through which it has passed.[1] Suppose that a batch of 100 units of partly manufactured type A has passed through department 1 and is awaiting treatment in department 2. We value the time consumed in department 1 at the standard direct labour cost plus the overhead cost, i.e. at £3.4 + £5.0 = £8.4 (Tables 6.2 and 6.3). Assume that the direct material cost of materials X and Y was incurred in cost centre 1— i.e. that when the job leaves cost centre 1, all the direct material to be used has already been issued except material Z. This allows us to add £77.9 for raw material cost (Table 6.1). The value of the 100 units of partly finished type A can then be assessed at £8.4 + £77.9 = £86.3. It is thus possible to build up an aggregate valuation, based on the materials issued and work done, priced at standard rates, for partly or wholly finished goods.

This kind of valuation does not produce, and is not intended to produce, an estimate of the saleable market value of the work-in-progress or finished goods. A standard cost valuation provides an approximate indicator of the extent to which resources on the average are absorbed in producing given units of output.

Some businesses value their work-in-progress and finished goods on the basis of the direct or 'prime' cost, making no addition for overhead cost. In the example just given, the work-in-progress would be valued by adding the direct labour cost to the direct material cost: £3.4 + £77.9 = £81.3. By this convention, overhead cost is not assumed to add to value and is, from a balance sheet point of view, treated as a reduction in the ownership claim— it is, so to speak, assumed to be completely lost as soon as it is spent. This convention does not affect the final profit in the longer run, but may affect its timing, whether in the budgets or in the actual accounts, because the whole of the overhead cost is treated as reduction of profit. If, on the other hand, the overhead cost is assumed to add value to the product, a net rise (say) in work-in-

[1] The valuation principle is the same, whether we are concerned with the construction of budgets, or of accounts for the actual results.

progress, or in the unsold finished goods, will absorb part of the overhead cost for the period. 'Direct costing' has the advantage of simplifying the accounting work, but it has not been widely adopted. (Possible reasons for this will be discussed in Chapter 7.)

The market value of work-in-progress will, in many businesses, be of little significance. Unless the work is such that another business can finish it as easily, or nearly as easily, as the business in which it has been produced, the market value will, in general, be lower than the minimum figure at which the management would be prepared to sell. In other words, the value of the work-in-progress to the business will in general be higher than the market value. This is another way of saying that it would not pay the business as a general policy to sell its partly finished work.

There are, however, exceptions. In certain types of business there may exist good markets for intermediate products, and in a given business the same may be true of some products and not of others. Material which has passed through one stage of a chemical process may be saleable in its own right. When an intermediate product enjoys a good market, the value in this market can reasonably be used for stock valuation purposes. The market values of finished or nearly finished goods, too, should be susceptible of close approximation. In practice, however, the market value method of valuation is not used very much for formal budgeting or accounting purposes, partly at least for traditional reasons.[1]

It may happen that a piece of work is clearly of less than standard value because of faulty material or workmanship. A certain proportion of spoilage can, indeed, usually be expected, and will be allowed for in the standard cost calculations: the planned total direct material, direct labour and overhead cost will be related to the production of good units of output. The sales value of spoiled units (other than those that will be re-processed) will be offset against the cost. In other words, the standard cost will be net of an allowance for the sale of scrap.

The reader will by now have realized that a standard cost is essentially what statisticians call a 'weight', that can be multiplied

[1] This does not mean that market values are ignored by the management. It may well be, however, that the traditional conventions need revision in this respect.

by the relevant physical quantities to produce an index of value. This index is an approximate, but only an approximate, indicator of the value of resources that have been, or will be, consumed in production. As a matter of fact the use of the word 'approximate' here can be disputed on the grounds that it suggests that accurate or precise figures could be found if only enough trouble were taken. This is not always true. In the case of expense that is allocated arbitrarily—e.g. the distribution of rent to departments, thence to cost centres, and thence to batches of product—there is no sense in which it can be said that such and such an allocation is 'correct' or 'accurate'. All that can be said is that the allocation serves, or does not serve, a useful purpose.[1]

Work-in-progress and finished goods budgets

If the production plan is sufficiently detailed, it may be possible to forecast the expected level of the physical work-in-progress throughout the year, and in particular at the end of each quarter, and value this. It may, however, be a good enough approximation for control purposes, and for estimating the output of finished goods, to calculate the budgeted work-in-progress by formula or by rule of thumb. Thus it might be assumed on the basis of previous experience that the work-in-progress at the end of any month would represent y per cent of total standard production cost incurred on the relevant product in the previous month. This kind of approximation may be quite close enough for normal budgeting, although of course it must be applied intelligently. If there were, for example, substantial changes in the period of production— the time from the starting of work on a product to its completion —the formula would have to be reconsidered. Or again, if production were rising or falling, or there were changes in the products, an established formula might be invalidated.

Let us assume that the standard value of the planned work-in-progress at the end of each quarter has been estimated. Let us also assume that the business is expected to be working to normal

---

[1] It may be noted here that if standard costs are not calculated, their place has to be taken by calculations that are even more arbitrary, in the sense of being less deliberately selected, e.g. based on the actual experience of the current year.

capacity.[1] Then for each quarter, and for the year, the budgeted standard value of opening work-in-progress *plus* the budgeted production cost in the period *minus* the budgeted standard value of closing work-in-progress (*plus*, for the quarterly figures only, an adjustment that will be explained below, called the budgeted calendar variance) will, by definition, give us the standard cost of the finished goods to be produced (Table 6.5). Row 1 of this table is identical with, and explained by, the bottom row of Table 5.5. The figure in the first and total columns of row 2 is the value of work-in-progress shown in the opening balance sheet (Table 3.1). The figure in the fourth and final columns of row 4 will appear in the estimated closing balance sheet. The final row contains the standard cost of the finished goods. This table reconciles the budgeted expenditure on production during the year with the standard value of the finished goods planned to be made available by the production process. It is, therefore, a budget of the changes in the (conventional) value of the asset 'work-in-progress'.

TABLE 6.5

WORK-IN-PROGRESS VALUE BUDGET 19—

	Jan. March	April– June	£ July– Sept.	Oct.– Dec.	Year
Production cost of output (Table 5.5) ..	80,365	82,840	67,138	69,659	300,002
Opening work-in-progress (Table 3.1) ..	12,410	14,166	12,638	11,573	12,410
	92,775	97,006	79,776	81,232	312,412
Closing work-in-progress ..	14,166	12,638	11,573	12,410	12,410
	78,609	84,368	68,203	68,822	300,002
Calendar variance	440	1,346	− 875	− 911	—
Standard production cost of finished goods	79,049	85,714	67,328	67,911	300,002

[1] This implies that the total overhead cost budgeted will be equal to the overhead content of the value of work produced, as measured by the cost centre allocations, and that no overhead cost will be 'lost'.

At the beginning of Chapter 5 we discussed the budgeting of the production of finished goods in physical quantities. We can now express the quantities of Table 5.1 in terms of value, using standard unit values. We can then summarize and re-arrange the figures to show the standard value of the goods planned to be sold during the year (Table 6.6): this is equal to the value of opening stocks (Table 3.1) *plus* the production for the year (Table 6.5) *less* the closing stock which will appear in the estimated closing balance sheet. This figure is called the 'cost of sales', and later will be set against the budgeted sales revenue of Table 4.1 to give the budgeted 'gross profit' for the year. The cost of sales is, from the point of view of balance sheet analysis, a fall in the ownership claim corresponding to the net outgo of finished goods to customers: Table 6.6 is the budget of changes in the (conventional) value of the asset 'finished goods'.

The fact that, for expository reasons, the budgets in Tables 6.5 and 6.6 appear here, does not imply that they are not drafted until the production planning discussed in Chapter 5 has been done. In fact the levels of work-in-progress and finished goods throughout the year are implied by, and enter into the calculation of, the production budget itself.

TABLE 6.6

FINISHED GOODS VALUE BUDGET 19—

	Jan.–March	April–June	£ July–Sept.	Oct.–Dec.	Year
Opening stock (Table 3.1) ..	12,449	27,716	35,812	5,152	12,449
Production (Table 6.5) ..	79,049	85,714	67,328	67,911	300,002
	91,498	113,430	103,140	73,063	312,451
Closing stock ..	27,716	35,812	5,152	11,734	11,734
Cost of sales ..	63,782	77,618	97,988	61,329	300,717

Calendar variance

We must now explain row 6 of Table 6.5.

A standard overhead rate per hour for a given cost centre, calculated by dividing the total annual normal hours available a that centre into the total budgeted overhead expense for the centre, will not necessarily be the same as that obtained by doing the same calculation for a given quarter. The annual expense may not accrue evenly over the quarters: heating and lighting for example is heavier in winter than in summer, and so on; furthermore, planned production in a given quarter may well not be one-quarter of the planned annual production. This gives rise to a 'calendar variance'.

We can show how calendar variance might affect the figures of our business. The planned production of finished goods of type A for the December quarter is 29,000 units (Table 5.1). The standard value of these units on the basis of the standard price of £1 10s. 7d. (Table 6.4) is £44,316. The corresponding figures for type B are 66,000 units and (we will assume) 7s. 2d., giving a standard value of production of £23,595. (These calculations are approximate, the standard unit cost shown in the text having been rounded off.) Thus, the total standard cost of production of finished goods in the December quarter is £44,316 + £23,595 = £67,911 (row 7 of Table 6.5). Now, the figures shown in the budgets for production cost in the December quarter (Table 5.5), when adjusted for work-in-progress changes, amount to £68,822 (Table 6.5). This differs from £67,911 by £911, which is the budgeted adverse calendar variance for the December quarter (row 6 of Table 6.5). This calendar variance is shown for each quarter in Table 6.5. For the whole year it disappears, the sum of the adverse variances in the last six months being equal to the sum of the favourable in the first six months. The variances arise from the (arbitrary) way in which the annual overhead cost has been allocated to the quarterly periods, and from variation from quarter to quarter in the annual rates of production.

We now turn to the control of production cost.

7

PRODUCTION—III

Control of production cost

In this chapter we shall consider first the budgetary control of production cost and of the stocks of work-in-progress and finished goods—the constant checking of the day-to-day results against the plans and standards.

It is the function of the accounting system to record and collect the figures that show the actual results and to arrange them in accounting statements in the same form as the budgets in order to facilitate comparison and analysis. Simplicity of presentation is one of the most important points in this work. The analysis and interpretation of the figures may, indeed, require a good deal of arithmetic. It is usually a mistake, however, to complicate the main summaries.

Table 7.1 shows the kind of statement that might be used to report the overall results of the production department. It shows the budgeted figures for the March quarter, with the actual figures reported, and the differences or variances.

TABLE 7.1

PRODUCTION COST REPORT
MARCH QUARTER 19—

	*Budget**	£ *Actual*	*Variance†*
Direct materials	48,037	54,695‡	− 6,658
Direct labour	20,512	22,635	− 2,123
Overhead	11,816	12,750	− 934
Total cost of work done ..	80,365	90,080	− 9,715
Standard hours of work done ..	(111,090)	(120,300)	(+ 9,210)

* *See* Table 6.5.

† Variances in which actual cost exceeds budgeted or standard cost or actual production is less than budgeted production are shown as negative in this and the following tables.

‡ Actual direct material cost is here the actual quantity used priced at the standard unit price.

One of the first questions that the management are likely to ask is how these figures are related to the physical production work planned and achieved in the quarter. A full answer requires a good deal of analysis. Hence it may be convenient to provide a first approximation. This is done in Table 7.1 by including, in row 5, the planned and actual standard hours equivalent of the work. These figures are the aggregates of the standard hours equivalent of the work done at the various cost centres. They provide a rough indicator of the level of physical production and thus give at a glance some idea of the use made of the production time available. They do not tell us how the output of the different products have varied among themselves. Nevertheless, a busy management may be prepared to accept a quick glance at such figures at frequent intervals as a means of deciding whether production in aggregate is going broadly according to plan, If, for example, there were a sharp increase in idle time in the workshops, there would be a corresponding fall in the actual standard hours of work shown in row 5. It must be remembered that these figures are only one of many sets of data that are continually coming into the hands of the management. All these data contribute in helping the management to maintain the 'feel' of the business—the general awareness of what is going on that is hard to define, but is very important.

If the general manager were reading Table 7.1 he would notice at once that the aggregate, and each element of, cost was higher than the budgeted figure and that the quantity of work done was also higher. These increases are consistent with the factory being busier than expected. He could ring up the production manager to confirm this impression, and ask whether the rise in production was sufficient to justify the rise in cost; he could also find out why production was higher, and make sure that it was justified by actual or expected sales. In this way quite a small number of figures, arranged in a significant way, could suggest to him questions, the answers to which in a few minutes would put him into closer touch with the march of business events. (It must be remembered that in practice he would probably have such figures at least monthly and perhaps weekly; it is not suggested that the general manager would not know until the end of the quarter that production was running at a higher level than budgeted.)

The production manager will want a more detailed analysis, and we must now consider how the variances can be analysed and interpreted. We shall, owing to restrictions of space, confine our study to the aggregate figures as shown in Table 7.1. This will allow us to discuss the principles involved. It is important in practice, however, to apply the same principles of analysis to detailed classes of cost, and to individual works departments and cost centres, in order to locate with precision the points where the variances arise. Indeed, most of the analysis will have to be done at this level in the first instance, the results being aggregated to give the figures for the production department as a whole.

The actual results can differ from the budgeted figures for a number of reasons. The level of output, the efficiency of production, the prices of raw materials, the wages of labour, the prices of services may all be different from those assumed in the original budget. A good system of control will distinguish these different factors from one another, so far as is possible.

Direct materials
Table 7.1 shows an adverse variance of £6,658 for direct materials. The first step in the analysis of this variance is to relate the actual production work done to the standard value of materials allowed for that work (calculated as in Chapter 6), thereby obtaining the standard direct material cost of the actual production work in the period. We shall assume this figure is £52,159. We can now say that part of the total variance, equal to the difference between this figure and the original budgeted cost of £48,037, i.e. £4,122, is explicable by a single cause, an increase in the volume of work. The next step is to compare the £52,159 standard cost of the actual production work with the standard value of materials actually used, which is recorded in Table 7.1 at £54,695. The difference between this figure and £52,159, £2,536, is the remainder of the variance. If we assume the standards are right, and that the quantities of materials used were valued at the standard prices,[1] as in the budgets,

---

[1] There is usually a 'price variance' to be explained too, due to the difference between the actual purchase price and the standard price. It is, in general, better to analyse price variances at the time the materials are bought, however; this will be discussed later.

the difference of £2,536 can only be due to excess usage of material, or to use of more expensive material than was planned. For this the production manager will want an explanation. As we shall see in Chapter 8, the accounting records can be arranged to show such variances as they occur from day-to-day and thus allow the enquiry to be made before the circumstances have been forgotten. The variance of £2,536 is called a quantity or usage variance because it reflects the value, at constant given prices, of variances from the standard quantities allowed.

We can express the preceding paragraph in a simple table that will tell the whole tale (Table 7.2).

TABLE 7.2
DIRECT MATERIAL VARIANCE ANALYSIS
MARCH QUARTER 19—

	£
Budgeted cost (Table 7.1)	48,037
Standard cost of actual work done	52,159
Variance allowed from original budget*	− 4,122
Standard cost of actual work done	52,159
Standard cost of actual usage (Table 7.1)	54,695
Quantity or usage variance	− 2,536
Total variance from original budget (Table 7.1)	− 6,658

* This variance is given a negative sign because it measures an increase in the cost compared with the original budget, but it is not adverse in the normal sense of the word since it is justified by increased production.

Control of material usage is particularly important in processes in which the material cost is a high proportion of the total value of the final product. Some firms find it worthwhile to control material costs closely even if they do not maintain a close control over labour or overhead cost.

Direct labour
We can analyse the variance between the original budgeted cost and the actual cost of direct labour into a part that is accounted for

by increased (or decreased) production, and a part that represents an excess (or deficiency) of actual cost above (or below) the standard allowance for the actual production. The original budgeted cost of direct labour is £20,512 (Table 7.1). Assume that the standard direct labour cost of the actual production work done (calculated as in Chapter 6) is £22,204. The difference between these figures, £1,692, is explained by the increase in the production work over the budgeted figure.

We now compare the standard cost of the actual production work, £22,204, with the actual cost of that work shown in Table 7.1, £22,635. The difference of £431 is an adverse variance due, if the standards are right, either (a) to actual wage rates being higher than the standard wage rates, or (b) to the time taken for the work done being longer than allowed in the standards, or (c) to a combination of (a) and (b). The next step accordingly is to divide the £431 into (a) the wage rate variance if any, and (b) what is usually called the efficiency variance, but could equally well be called the quantity or time variance. This analysis will be carried out in the first instance for each cost centre, the results being summed.

Let us consider the efficiency variance first. This is obtained by multiplying the standard hourly wage cost, first by the standard time relevant to the actual quantity of production achieved—the standard hour equivalent of the work which gives us the figure of £22,204 already mentioned, and secondly by the actual time taken for that production. We shall assume the second figure is £21,557. The difference between the two figures is the efficiency variance, here a favourable figure of £647. This is an indicator in value terms of the time that has been gained in production as compared with the standard time allowed. By using the standard wage cost per standard hour of production to value the time, we avoid the complication of any change in wage rates. The variance is, therefore, not necessarily an actual money saving: it is the saving that would have taken place if wage rates had remained at the level expected when the standards were set. The production manager will be closely concerned with efficiency variances, which in some sense reflect his own efficiency.

We now have to analyse the effect of differences between wage rates actually paid and the standard rates, while excluding the effect of time variances. For this we compare the cost of the actual time

D

taken, priced at the standard wage rates (already given above as £21,557), with the actual wage cost of the actual time taken (which is given in Table 7.1 as £22,635). The difference is an adverse variance of £1,078.

We have thus analysed the total variance of £2,123 shown in Table 7.1 into three components, each of which corresponds to a particular cause or class of causes that can be related to the responsibility of particular persons. The analysis is summarized simply and conveniently in Table 7.3.

The analysis does not stop at this point. Each of the separate variances must be investigated and explained. Thus the wage rate variance may be due to other causes than straightforward increases in wage rates, such as may arise, for example, from a national wage award. It may emerge because the type of labour used has been other than that laid down in the original standards. It may, therefore, be necessary to obtain reports of changes in the type of labour used in the various cost centres. From these it will be possible to calculate how much of any wage rate variance is due to the use of a more, or

TABLE 7.3

DIRECT LABOUR VARIANCE ANALYSIS
MARCH QUARTER 19—

	£
Budgeted cost (Table 7.1)	20,512
Standard cost of actual work done	22,204
Variance allowed from original budget*	− 1,692
Standard cost of actual work done	22,204
Standard cost of actual hours worked	21,557
Efficiency variance	+ 647
Standard cost of actual hours worked	21,557
Actual cost of actual hours worked (Table 7.1)	22,635
Wage rate variance	− 1,078
Total variance from original budget (Table 7.1)	− 2,123

* *See* footnote to Table 7.2.

less, expensive type of labour than had been planned. The interpretation of the wage rates variance may also require reference back to the efficiency variance. The use of more expensive labour might, for example, result in an adverse wage rate variance, but produce a favourable efficiency variance. As always, it is dangerous to interpret any single figure by itself without considering its effect on other figures.

It is also possible that what is, in effect, a change in wage rates, may occur as a result of some kind of wage incentive system. Suppose that payment was by direct piece rate, so that the rate paid varied in direct proportion to production. Suppose also that the efficiency achieved was below 100 per cent, the actual time taken for a given piece of production being greater than the standard time. An adverse efficiency variance would then be shown. On the other hand, the actual cost per hour *of the hours worked* would be less than the standard hourly rate. (The standard wage rate would be based on the assumption of normal, i.e. standard, efficiency.) The wage rate variance would then be favourable, and would exactly offset the adverse efficiency variance. Again, efficiency might be so low that payment was based, not upon the piece rate, but on the minimum guaranteed hourly rate. In this case the adverse efficiency variance would not be completely offset by an equivalent reduction in the hourly cost rate.

A wage rate variance can also arise if overtime payments are made. Provision can be made for reporting the amounts involved so that the effect of these too can be distinguished and their cause investigated.

One of the reasons why it is desirable to separate the efficiency variance from the wage rate variance is that a fall in efficiency implies that the fixed resources of the business are being used less economically. If expensive equipment is in use and jobs take longer than expected it is very desirable that this should be brought to light early. Calculating a labour efficiency variance from day to day— possibly on a time basis only, without valuing at the standard rate the hours gained or lost—is one of the ways of dealing with this problem. As in the case of direct materials, the most effective way of controlling the variances is to arrange for reports to be made from day to day. In this way the efficiency variance can be built up daily, and separated from the wage rate variance. One would expect that when a report of the kind set out in Table 7.3 was sent to the production manager he would be able to obtain, if he wished, a detailed analysis in a form that would go a long way towards answering his question: 'In what department and on what days did these variances arise and what was their apparent cause?'

Overhead cost

We start with the important concept of the flexible budget. This is, in principle, a set of schedules relating the expected level of overhead cost to different levels and types of physical production work. Once the actual work done in a period is known, a total 'allowed cost' can be obtained from the schedules. The original overhead budget approved for the period can be regarded as one of the sets of figures that comprise the flexible budget—the set appropriate to the planned physical production.[1] We shall assume that the flexible budget schedules, when calculated, show the allowed cost for the March quarter, based on the production work done, to be £12,623. The difference of £807 between this and the budgeted cost of £11,816 (Table 7.1) reflects the expected increase in cost from the rise in production as compared with the budgeted figure. This variance is justified by the increased production and is not the responsibility of the production manager, unless he has produced more than has been agreed, in which case it is not the variance itself but the failure to keep to plan that is relevant.

The difference between the allowed cost—the flexible budget cost of the actual work done—and the actual cost incurred is, however, the responsibility of the production manager and for this reason is sometimes called the 'controllable variance'. It is analogous to the labour efficiency and wage rate variances, and the material usage variance, and as with these, the responsibility of the production manager is not to be interpreted to mean that all variances are necessarily his fault. The actual overhead cost of the work done in the March quarter was £12,750 (Table 7.1). Hence the controllable variance was £127, the difference between £12,623 and £12,750. This

[1] But the acceptance of the principle of flexible budgeting does not mean that the actual schedules always exist: it is more likely that they will be calculated as needed.

is an adverse variance, actual cost being above the allowed flexible budget figure. It is a fairly small figure, however, and might not be thought worthy of special investigation. If it were investigated—and a small difference may conceal large partially compensating differences—it would be necessary to scan the detailed expense classifications that made up the total figures, in order to locate the classes of expenditure in which the main differences between the flexible budget schedules and the actual accounting data had occurred.

The analysis just described can be summarized conveniently as shown in Table 7.4.

The construction of the flexible budget requires the study of the many different types of expense and their behaviour in relation to output. Some expenses vary, in a greater or less degree, with the time occupied in production at particular cost centres or works departments—power, heating, lighting, for example, may fall into this category. Other expenses, such as cleaning materials, oil, screws, nails and so on, vary with the output of particular products. A third group remain constant, unaffected over relatively large ranges of output by the time used on production or by the level of output. Such expenses are rent, rates and insurance of premises—though these, too, will jump upwards or downwards if there is a sufficiently large change in output capacity. Schedules are worked out relating expenses that vary with production time to hours of working at the

TABLE 7.4

PRODUCTION OVERHEAD VARIANCE ANALYSIS
MARCH QUARTER 19—

	£
Budgeted cost (Table 7.1)	11,816
Flexible budget allowance for work done	12,623
Variance allowed from original budget*	— 807
Flexible budget allowance for work done	12,623
Actual cost (Table 7.1)	12,750
Controllable variance	— 127
Total variance from original budget (Table 7.1)	— 934

* See footnote to Table 7.2.

various cost centres, and expenses that vary with output to the different levels of output of the various products. Constant expenses are estimated separately. Once these calculations have been made, the allowed cost for a particular output combination can be built up by aggregating the different types of cost.

If the production processes for the different products are similar, it may be possible to build up a schedule relating the total overhead cost in each works department, or possibly in the works as a whole, to the standard hours of production time. The allowed cost can then be read off in each period as soon as the standard hours equivalent of work produced are known. This kind of simplification implies that a fairly constant relationship between quantities of different products produced will hold, since a standard hour's work on one product will not necessarily affect cost by the same amount as a standard hour on another: they may not use the same machines, and the expenses that are functions of quantity processed may not be related in the same way to standard hours of production as those that are functions of time.

The essential idea is to obtain the best estimate of the cost related to each level of output of each of the various products. There is a cost in costing, and it will not be worth while refining the figures if to do so costs more than the information is believed to be worth. Since one of the major functions of the analysis is to make people think about what is going on in the factory, it may be sufficient to use quite rough figures provided the limitations are properly understood. Like all such tools, the flexible budget is not a precision instrument. However carefully it is prepared, it will be in some degree arbitrary, and it must be used accordingly. When the actual overhead costs reported for a period are interpreted by comparing them with the flexible budget, and seeking for the explanations of differences, it is essential to keep in mind the way in which the budget was prepared: the circumstances for which it is valid must be known. If the pattern of production changes so radically that the assumptions on which it was prepared no longer hold good, the comparison of actual expenditure with the flexible budget must be abandoned in favour of control by *ad hoc* analysis, that is by considering the various classes of actual expense in relation to *ad hoc* estimates of what they should have been.

The separate control of direct material and direct labour costs is really a special application of the flexible budget principle to these two special classes of cost. The assumption that these costs vary in direct proportion to output is a convenient first approximation for the purpose of analysis.

The formal preparation of flexible budget data is not always necessary. It may often be found convenient to control overhead cost by a simple comparison of actual expenditure with the original budget estimates. Provided that the total cost is sub-classified adequately into the various types of expense, it will often be a relatively simple matter to trace serious divergencies between the original budget and the actual figures, and explain these.

If a flexible budget is used it will require annual (and perhaps more frequent) revision. This revision will normally form part of the process of preparing or revising the annual budget so far as this relates to overhead cost.

Control of work-in-progress and finished goods

There is not a great deal to add, with respect to the budgetary control of the levels of the stocks of work-in-progress and finished goods, to what has already been said in Chapter 6. The normal accounting reports will include statements of the values of these stocks, and will compare these with the budget estimates of Tables 6.5 and 6.6. The management will naturally be concerned with any substantial variances between the budgeted levels of stocks (as amended for any change in plans) and the actual levels, since these may indicate, for example (if stocks are lower than expected), that production is running at a lower level than planned, or that the production plan has not been amended to deal with an increased sales demand, or (if stocks are higher than expected) that bottle-necks are occurring in production, leading to an unplanned build-up in work-in-progress, or that sales are lower than was expected and that production has not been cut back enough, and so on. It will be necessary to arrange for reports on the quality and value of any stocks that do not seem likely to sell at the originally budgeted prices. These will be reduced in value for profit calculation and for balance sheet purposes. In order to distinguish variances between the actual and the budgeted figures due to different causes, these value adjustments should be reported separately, standard unit costs being used for valuation purposes in the comparisons of the actual with the budgeted stocks.

As it is often convenient to value the actual physical production on the basis of the unit standard costs, and as the total actual production cost in any given period is seldom likely to coincide with the standard value of production so calculated, it is necessary to report the difference as a variance, representing a loss or profit arising from the excess or shortfall of actual cost as compared with the standard allowance. If the production is valued for accounting purposes at the standard *direct* cost, excluding all overhead cost (which is then treated as if it were an ancillary expense or 'loss' and did not add to the value of production), this variance is merely the sum of the direct material and labour variances already described in Tables 7.2 and 7.3.

If the unit overhead cost is also included when the production is valued (as in our budgets), the variance will also be explained in part by the controllable overhead variance as calculated in Table 7.4. However, this will probably not explain the whole difference, for the flexible budget cost normally moves less than in proportion to output whereas the valuation of production at standard unit overhead cost implies that total overhead cost moves in direct proportion to output; i.e. multiplying production work done by its standard unit cost will, in general, produce a figure in excess of (or below) the flexible budget cost as production is above (or below) normal. This remaining difference is sometimes called a volume variance, because it shows the effect of changes in the volume of production on cost that is relatively fixed per unit of output. (When parts of the year are concerned there may also be a calendar variance element, which can be analysed separately.)

Opportunity cost
Up to now we have been considering the budgets as an expression of planning decisions for a given period, the main object of which is to establish an annual operational plan and maintain control over the business operation. We could indeed call these budgets the 'control budgets'. We now consider briefly the relation between the budgeting and accounting data and the other economic decisions that are constantly being made in business.

under review so that they reflect the current management decisions. Similarly he must see that the probable effect of such decisions on the annual budgets are clear when the decisions are being made. The business standing orders must, therefore, ensure that he participates in, or is consulted on, such decisions. The annual budgets provide the framework within which the day-to-day administrative decisions are made, and set the limits of action which can only be crossed by obtaining formal approval for a budget alteration from the general manager or the board of directors, as the importance of the decision and the standing orders require. In this way the general management can retain control.

Allocation of overhead costs

We shall conclude this chapter by discussing a matter concerning which there has been, and still is, a good deal of controversy.

In Chapter 6 we saw how, on the basis of certain assumptions, the total production overhead costs can be divided up and 'allocated' in such a way that standard overhead cost rates can be calculated for each unit of each product. This kind of calculation is made in many businesses. If standard costs are not in use it is common to find that the data shown in the accounting system are similarly analysed to produce the 'actual cost' for each unit of product in a given period. Now, this kind of calculation does not produce figures that can tell us the difference in cost that will result from producing more or less of any given unit of product, for it is arrived at by including expenses that do not vary in direct proportion to output and by allocating on an arbitrary basis, to the different products, expenses that contribute to more than one product. It is therefore interesting to ask why such allocations are so often made, the more so since they necessarily lead to increased complications in the costing system.

There is little doubt that a good deal of this kind of work is a matter of habit, encouraged by uncritical text-books. It has been customary for calculations of this kind to be made in the past, accountants and other business men have become used to seeing them, and as a result they like to go on seeing them. There are, however, other reasons.

It may be argued that the allocation of common overhead costs to cost centres, and thence to individual products in order to obtain unit product costs, can help the control of operations in the following way. Suppose the planned output of all products for a period has been determined, and a calculation has been made spreading the whole of the budgeted overhead cost among the products, as in the examples in Chapter 6. Then the management know that, provided they sell the budgeted output of each product at a price not less than the direct cost *plus* the overhead cost so calculated *plus* the planned profit margin per unit, at least the planned profit will be achieved. With this picture in their minds they can concentrate their attention on the actual unit costs as these are reported, interpreting any variances in these from the budget estimates in terms of their effect on the total budgeted profit. It is doubtful whether this approach—which may involve a good deal of clerical work—provides any control that is not equally obtainable from studies based on the flexible budget and the principle of control by difference. It will almost certainly be harder to understand and explain to members of the staff who are not used to the system—a serious defect, since it is very important that the technical staff should be kept in close touch with accounting data. However, some people may prefer to do their thinking in this way; if it helps them this is a good enough reason for using the method, provided other people are not unduly hindered, and that the cost of the extensive allocation of overhead cost that may be required is not overlooked.

It has been suggested that a carefully calculated allocation of overhead cost may be of value in planning by indicating the extent to which particular manufacturing operations utilize more or less expensive resources. Suppose product A takes up twice as much time on expensive machines as product B. In the longer run at least, an increase in the production of A may require the purchase of more machines than would otherwise have been necessary. Hence A is in the longer run more expensive to produce (so far as time on these machines is concerned) even though in the short run once the machines have been bought their use for A rather than B may have very little effect on their saleable value or their future services to the business. By allocating a proportion of the depreciation of the machines to the products, on a time-in-use basis (as discussed in Chapter 6), the greater long run costliness of A may be emphasized. This is certainly a way of dealing with a factor—the relevance of far as possible show when there is a transfer of resources from one responsible person to another) will be devised to show when material of a given value has moved from the control of the storekeeper to, say, the control of a production foreman. This can be done by sending the accounting department a copy of the list of material issued. The accounts are then adjusted to show, e.g. in the case of an issue for production, an increase in the value of the asset 'work-in-progress' and a decrease in the value of the asset 'stock of raw material'.

The accounting records are cross-referenced to the order or form which is the formal authority for the transaction. These original documents are preserved and are available for inspection, e.g. by the auditors, if later it becomes necessary to check the accounting records.

If a standard costing system is in use the accounting organization will provide, as explained already, for a comparison of the standard direct material cost of products with the standard cost of actual issues. One of the most effective ways of maintaining such a check is to require special authorization of any stores issued in excess of the standard allowance. Excess issues can then be reported as they occur.

If the raw materials in store are valued for accounting purposes at their standard prices no question of price variances—variances due to differences between standard prices and actual prices—arises at this stage. These are dealt with when the material is purchased. This is the simplest procedure if it is practicable. If, however, the stock is valued for accounting purposes at 'actual cost' (that is, at a figure derived by some kind of averaging of the original purchase price of different lots), the difference between this value and the value obtained by pricing the same quantity at the standard price, is calculated and reported at this stage. This difference is the price variance.

The accounting system not only deals with the reporting of variances as they arise, so that immediate attention is drawn to them; it also provides for their accumulation so that the summarized direct material consumption of each period can be analysed into a standard allowance, and variances, as shown in Chapter 7.[1]

[1] Indirect material control comes under the head of overhead cost, below.

Accounting for labour

The essential accounting distinction between labour and material is that labour cannot be stored. It is possible to make a distinction between controlling material in store that is waiting to be used (*see* Chapter 11) and controlling the actual use of material. This distinction does not arise in the case of labour. The accounting procedure for labour cost can be divided into two main parts. First, there is the procedure for calculating the amounts that are due to all the employees for each period, deducting income tax, national insurance payments, contributions to trade unions and national saving schemes, etc., ensuring that all these deductions are paid over in due course to the appropriate authority, ensuring that payment is not made to non-existent people, and controlling the actual wage payment to ensure that cash is not lost or stolen. Secondly, there is the process of analysing the wage cost in order to compare the actual expenditure with the standards, and in general to relate cost to work achieved.

It is not possible in the space available to discuss the necessary organization in detail. All that can be done is to indicate in general terms what arrangements have to be made. The payments will be determined by individual contract, wage regulations and negotiated wage agreements. If payment is based, wholly or partly, on time rates it is necessary to ensure that the worker has been available for the contracted time. This is usually done by arranging for some kind of time recording at the entrance to factories or to works departments, showing when each person arrived and left. The information obtained from these records is collated in the accounting department and the pay due is then calculated. If payment is wholly or partly related to the work done, i.e. there is some kind of piece rate or bonus system in force, these time records, if they are kept at all, have to be supplemented by detailed information from the works departments. The records from the different departments have to be analysed and summarized so that the total work done by each person on different jobs can be agreed with his overall time record. From these two groups of records and the information about the basic wage rates, i.e. the relationship between time worked and/or output achieved and payment, the gross wage due is calculated.

The net pay is then calculated from known information about the income tax position of each employee, and of other deductions. This provides the information which allows the pay packets to be prepared, and the total amount of cash needed to be withdrawn from the bank.

The difference between the net payment made to the employee and the gross pay due is eventually paid over to the particular organizations for whose benefit the deductions have been made. Until then the accounts must record a liability to each of these organizations. From the point of view of the business, the cost of the labour is the total amount paid or to be paid.

The time and piece rate records provide the data for analysing the gross wage cost into the various accounting classifications, so that the direct wage cost can be related to the relevant production and the indirect wage cost, including the wage cost of idle time, can be classified as in the flexible budget. The analysis of the direct labour variances can be maintained continuously by relating the time and wage rate data for each production order to the standard allowances specified by that order. In this way variances are brought to light at once and an explanation of the total direct labour cost variance for each period is available at the end of the period.

The cost of maintaining a complete wage cost analysis is fairly high and some businesses will be content to maintain a continuous check on performance times without going to the length of calculating variances in money values every week. In such cases, the detailed periodic variance analysis discussed in Chapter 7 may be replaced by a rougher *ad hoc* analysis.

The overall accounting control over labour cost is maintained by recording, in the formal double-entry accounting system, a reduction in the asset 'cash at bank' when the wages are paid, together with an increase in liabilities in respect of deductions from wages not yet paid over to the appropriate recipient, and a corresponding increase in the asset 'work-in-progress' or in one of the various classes of expense which are not assumed to add to the value of production, as the case may be.[1] This means the value for which the cashier is accountable has been reduced and there is an equivalent

---

[1] The latter will include variances from standard cost and, if 'direct costing' is in use, all indirect labour cost.

rise in the total, in the form of stock value or of expense not allocated to specific production, for which the production manager is now accountable.

Accounting for production overhead cost

The accounting system must, if it is to fulfil its purpose, sub-classify the overhead cost by fields of responsibility, and by types of expense within each field, so that reports can be supplied to those responsible for each field and so that the general management can be kept informed of the expenditure in all sections. This system of classification must be the same as the system used for budgeting.

The information about factory overhead cost comes through three main channels. The cost of indirect materials is obtained from the reports of stores issued. The authority to issue will be given as the occasion demands, or as a standing order for a specified daily, weekly or monthly issue.

The information for the analysis of the indirect wage cost will be obtained from the original wage accounting records in the same way as the direct labour cost data.

The accounting control of general expense[1] divides itself into the two main heads of (a) ensuring that the cash payments, when made, reach the supplier from whom services have been received; and (b) ensuring that the amounts to be paid correspond with the services received.

The first of these problems will be considered in Chapter 11. The second is dealt with by requiring heads of works departments, or subordinates they have delegated for the purpose, to approve the bills from suppliers before these are recorded as liabilities by entry in the formal accounts. This acts as a check on the correctness of the payment and on the fact that the services for which the payment is made have indeed been received. It is also the authority, from the departmental head to the accounting department, to charge the sum concerned to an account for which he is responsible. He is thus in the position at all times to know, or to be able to ascertain, the expenditure that is being debited to such accounts. This is important. Unless the departmental head is in the position to verify the payments for which he is being held responsible, he may well

[1] Other than depreciation, discussed elsewhere.

feel that he has no control over the actions of the accounting department and be inclined to dispute expenditure which he is asked to explain. The duties of the accounting staff are arranged to ensure that this procedure is followed.

Once stores have been issued, or money paid for wages or general expense (or a liability to pay money recognized), the storekeeper, the cashier, or the clerk responsible for liabilities, will be given credit in the formal double-entry accounting system to indicate that they have so much less to account for, or, in the case of liabilities, that they can call on the cashier for settlement. The production manager now has to justify the outlay so far as it represents a departure from the figure allowed in the flexible budget.

Work-in-progress

The work-in-progress in the factory must be under accounting control to reduce the chance that valuable work and stores will be lost or stolen, or sent to customers without notification being given to the accounts department so that the customer can be invoiced and the debt collected. If there is standard costing, the control is maintained by building up a record of the standard direct material, labour and, if required, overhead cost of the production operations as they are performed. The aggregate standard cost thus recorded provides a continuing value indicator of the work-in-progress for which the production department is responsible.

This record is linked in the accounting system with the release of the cashier, storekeeper, etc., from responsibility as the cash is paid for wages and the stores are issued for production, etc. So far as the actual costs represented by these payments and issues exceed, or are less than, the standard cost of the work done, variances are recorded and these are summed and reported independently. The accounting record can be proved at any time by checking the physical-work-in-progress and valuing it on the basis of its standard cost. As we have already emphasized it is not essential for this control that an overhead allocation system be in force. The control can be maintained by pricing the work-in-progress on the basis of the standard cost of direct materials and labour—'prime cost'. If there is no standard costing system the control (if any) has to be maintained by recording the actual cost incurred on the work of each production order.

Finished goods

As work-in-progress is finished and is transferred from the production floor to the finished goods store, or is sent to the customer, the accounting department is notified and the record of responsibility shifted in the double-entry accounting system from the production department to the finished goods storekeeper. The value of work-in-progress is reduced (credited) and that of finished goods increased (debited) in the formal accounts. The balance of the finished goods account should always tally with the value of the goods in the store. This can be checked by physical inspection. A constant accounting control can be maintained by making periodic physical checks on the quantities of goods in store, valuing these, and comparing the results with the balance recorded in the accounts. This can be done, if necessary, on a statistical sampling basis.

The notification that the goods have been despatched to customers will initiate accounting entries crediting the storekeeper and debiting the account of the customer, thus creating a new asset equal to the sales value of the goods. The clerks responsible for controlling debts outstanding will be responsible for ensuring that money is in due course received from the debtor. This also implies a net change, normally an increase, in the shareholders' claim, representing a net increase in asset values—the difference between the standard cost of the goods sold (credited to the storekeeper) and the selling value (debited to the customer). This is a component of the profit or loss for the year.

We now turn to the budgets relating to the miscellaneous overhead costs that are not the responsibility of the production manager.

9

MISCELLANEOUS OVERHEAD COSTS

General

In this chapter we discuss the costs that arise in connection with selling and distribution activities, research and development and the general administration of the business. Under the usual accounting conventions these outlays and the remaining current outlays to be discussed in Chapter 10, the non-production overhead costs, do not add to the recorded value of the work-in-progress or finished goods, that is, they are regarded from the point of view of balance sheet analysis as a reduction in the ownership claim. (They are thus on the same footing as production overhead cost in a system of direct costing in which unsold output is valued at prime cost only.) Much of what has already been said with respect to the production over-head cost applies to these costs, and the discussion will therefore be directed mainly towards special points. As usual, each budget must be consistent with the planned physical activities of the department to which it relates, and both the budget and the activities must be consistent with all the other budgets and activities of the company. The budgets are drafted by, or in co-operation with, the appropriate departmental managers, and finally agreed by them, and there must be close co-operation between departments; the figures that emerge finally will almost certainly be the result of a series of adjustments, reflecting the process of getting all the budgets into step.

The control of the expense is carried out, as usual, by comparing the actual expense from period to period with the original budget figures. For this it is normally necessary to analyse the budgeted and actual expense in considerable detail.

One of the budgeting difficulties is that it is not usually easy to establish any close relationship between expenditure of the kind we are now discussing and its results in terms of increased revenue or reduced cost elsewhere in the business and there are certain kinds of outlay—e.g. the advertising of products—concerning which it is sometimes almost wholly a matter of faith whether or not they are worthwhile. The budgeting procedure does, however, ensure that the various expenses come under at least annual scrutiny, and sets a limit to the expense that can be incurred without further authority from the general management.

Selling and distribution

Table 9.1 is the selling and distribution cost budget for our business. It includes such expenses as the salaries of the selling staff (but not the sales manager, who is not responsible for his own salary), advertising, travelling, postage and telephone, delivery expenses, stationery and printing, and so on, so far as these are the responsibility of the sales manager.

The expenses shown in the last two rows of the budget before the totals are of a rather different nature from the others. Cash discounts do not represent money payments; they are reductions that some businesses allow to their customers in their debts, provided they pay before a certain specified date, the reduction in the cash collected from customers being offset by the fact that the cash comes in earlier and thus saves interest. The granting of cash discounts is

TABLE 9.1

SELLING AND DISTRIBUTION COST BUDGET 19—

	Jan.–March	April–June	July–Sept.	Oct.–Dec.	Year
			£		
Staff	2,700	2,700	2,700	2,700	10,800
Advertising ..	900	10,900	900	900	13,600
Travelling and Communication	1,125	1,295	1,465	1,115	5,000
Delivery	561	642	737	560	2,500
General	360	360	360	360	1,440
	5,646	15,897	6,162	5,635	33,340
Cash discounts ..	206	215	371	200	992
Bad debts ..	500	500	500	500	2,000
	6,352	16,612	7,033	6,335	36,332

closely connected with the prices and other terms on which the sales are made, and is likely, therefore, to be under the control of the sales manager. It is possible to allocate cash discounts approximately to quarters or months because they will be related to the amounts of the debts outstanding at the beginning of each quarter or month: it will usually be possible to estimate from past experience, modified by any changes in selling conditions, how much of these debts will be paid early enough for the discount to be granted.

The money to be received from customers in respect of sales may also be reduced by bad debts. It is the experience of most businesses selling on credit that a certain number of these will be incurred. In any given year, therefore, it is necessary to make some kind of estimate of the expected amount. These, too, are not independent of selling policy. For example, a strong sales campaign, taking the company's business into areas where it had not been before, could conceivably result in a substantial increase in the percentage of bad debts, at least for the time being. It is, therefore, relevant to consider bad debts, too, in relation to the responsibility of the sales manager. It should be noted, however, that the actual collection of the debts may not be under his control; this may, and probably will, be the function of the accounting department under the controller. This has to be remembered when any variances are interpreted.

The calculation of the expected amount of the bad debts may be based upon statistical evidence from the past, or upon a detailed scrutiny of the individual debts at the beginning of the year; in practice it is likely that the two methods will be combined. The allocation of expected bad debts to quarters or months will necessarily be a rather rougher exercise than the estimation of cash discounts.

Research and development cost
Some companies must carry on expenditure on research and development if they are to maintain their business; if they do not do so other businesses will produce better or cheaper products, and they will gradually fall behind. Others may be interested in expanding their business, or in the nature of the research itself, even if there is no great economic pressure on them. From the point of view of its construction, this budget differs little from the other overhead cost

budgets. It has, however, a special characteristic due to the nature of the work to which it relates: expenditure envisaged in the production budget is expected, if all goes well, to produce a certain quantity of goods of a fairly well defined type and quality; the probable results of expenditure on research and, to a lesser extent, development, are likely to be less clearly visible and, like advertising expenditure, the outlay may be to a considerable extent a matter of faith.

This characteristic of research and development cost means that, though the problem of maintaining consistency with the other budgets still exists, the conditions will in certain respects be less stringent. The budget as a whole must still be consistent with the finance budget so that the necessary money will be available when wanted. The physical development work, and perhaps some of the research work, must no doubt tie in with the general longer-term business forecast on which all the budgets are in part based. Sometimes, however, the outlay will be linked with the other budgets only through the finance budget.

Although the exact results which are likely to come from expenditure on research and development are on the whole rather vague, once the budget has been laid down it is not difficult to control the expenditure in the sense of checking whether the actual expenditure under each classified head of expense is greater or less than appears in the original budget. It is, however, of the nature of the work that variances are particularly likely to arise in respect of particular heads of expense, even if the overall budget is fulfilled fairly closely. It is, in fact, likely that considerable discretion will be given to the head of this department in amending his original budget classifications. One would expect no great fuss to be made if rather more was expended on labour than had been expected, and rather less on materials, rather more on project X and rather less on Y, and so on. One would also expect, however, that there would be certain limits to the amount of change which would be allowed without formal approval by the general management. Furthermore, the total expenditure allowed would be limited by the budget and any substantial variance over the total figures month by month would no doubt be investigated. It would, however, often be hard to decide whether the variance was or was not justified. In this kind of situation the general management of the business are very much in the hands of their research and development staff, and the effectiveness of the control must depend, even more than usual, on good personal relationships, on close personal contact, and on a belief that if one appoints a person for a given activity it is as well to trust him while he is doing that activity until he has proved that he cannot do it.

The general accounting arrangements for research and development are likely to be much the same as for the other budgets. The formal accounting records will be no different in principle. The actual collection and classification of the data may, however, be rather more difficult because research staff are unlikely to be working in fairly stereotyped ways and hence it will not be so easy to obtain a systematic record of materials, labour time, etc. devoted to particular subjects. Perhaps one of the best ways of overcoming this difficulty is to make sure that the accounting staff in contact with the research staff are sympathetic to the kind of work that the latter are doing. If you point out to the head of a research and development department that the figures which are going into the accounts are, in effect, no more than a statistical check, susceptible in some degree to the kind of scientific investigation that he himself is carrying out in relation to the products of the business, he is likely to be co-operative. Here as always, however, the 'cost of

TABLE 9.2

RESEARCH AND DEVELOPMENT COST
BUDGET 19—

	Jan.–March	April–June	July–Sept.	Oct.–Dec.	Year
Staff	1,320	1,320	1,320	1,320	5,280
Labour	960	960	960	960	3,840
Materials	1,890	1,890	1,890	1,890	7,560
Communication	120	120	120	120	480
General	420	420	420	420	1,680
	4,710	4,710	4,710	4,710	18,840
Depreciation:					
Equipment	180	180	180	180	720
Building	210	210	210	210	840
	5,100	5,100	5,100	5,100	20,400

costing' must be balanced against the usefulness of the additional information which it is thought will be obtained from the cost records.

The summary research and development budget for our business is shown in Table 9.2.

General administration cost
We shall use this budget (Table 9.3) as a residual category embracing all the remaining current expenses except the salaries of the various heads of the main departments and the general manager, the directors' fees, the financial expenses and taxation, all of which will be dealt with in Chapter 10. We may assume this budget to be the responsibility of the controller himself. In practice, particularly in a large business, there would probably be many overhead cost budgets not described separately here, each representing a classification or sub-classification of responsibility. There is, however, little to be gained from the point of view of illustrating general principles in multiplying the number of such budgets discussed.

No doubt many general administration outlays will be incurred for the benefit to a greater or lesser degree of other departments. However, the responsibility for every expense must be allotted to one person and, as we have already said, provided the interdependence of business activities is understood, the figures need not be misinterpreted. All departmental heads will presumably have the opportunity of discussing this problem at the time when the budgets are being drawn up and it is at this stage that they must draw attention to implications of other people's budgets for their own departments.

It is a matter of choice to what extent expense that relates to a number of departments should be sub-divided and allocated to the budgets of the different departments on some more or less arbitrary basis. If, for example, the general administration section is providing services—accounting, building-space, etc.—for other departments, there is something to be said for showing in its budget a recovery of cost from the departments which have had the services, i.e. to record a revenue in the general administration budget and a corresponding expense in the other relevant budgets. For example, the general overhead cost shown in Table 9.3 might be a net figure after

TABLE 9.3

GENERAL ADMINISTRATION COST BUDGET 19—

£

	Jan.–March	April June	July–Sept.	Oct.–Dec.	Year
Staff	2,250	2,250	2,250	2,250	9,000
Communication..	201	201	201	201	804
Maintenance ..	130	130	130	130	520
General	210	210	210	241	871
	2,791	2,791	2,791	2,822	11,195
Depreciation:					
Equipment ..	300	300	300	300	1,200
Buildings ..	39	39	39	39	156
	3,130	3,130	3,130	3,161	12,551

bringing in an imputed 'receipt' from the selling and distribution and other departments for the cost of accounting for their activities. These departments' general overheads in turn would include a corresponding imputed 'payment'.

One of the points in favour of charging each department notionally with all the services it uses, even though it is not primarily responsible for the payment for these services, is that it brings to the attention of the manager of that department the fact that he is using a particular resource and suggests to him that he may be able to economize by using less. It would for example be open to the sales manager, if he were charged with rent for the space he was occupying, to say that he could hire cheaper space himself in some other building. Not only does this make the sales manager constantly aware of the fact that he should be looking around to see whether he can get accommodation more cheaply elsewhere. It also has the effect of making the general administration, who provide the accommodation, consider whether or not they are doing so on the best basis. It is this constant drawing of attention to different facets of the business, to the different kinds of resources that are being used, and to the different kinds of revenue that are being received, that helps to justify a budgeting system.

Depreciation cost is often less closely related to departmental activities than other cost. This is particularly the case with assets like office buildings, where the intensity of use is not likely to make very much difference to the life or value. It might be argued, therefore, that there is not much point in putting the depreciation of buildings into these budgets. The advantage of including this figure is that we draw attention to the existence of a particular kind of expense which is continuing all the time; even though our estimate of the amount is by its nature not very precise, the depreciation is an indicator that the building is being used and is therefore absorbing some resources which would otherwise be available for other uses; it is a reminder. This is true *a fortiori* of depreciation of such equipment as office machinery. This kind of asset is shorter lived than a building, and will probably wear out more quickly if it is used heavily. It is, therefore, all the more important that the expense, even though it is a rough estimate, should be included in the budget.

The comparison of the general administration expense budget with the actual results, month by month and quarter by quarter, will be carried out in exactly the same way as with the other departments.

The accounting records
The accounting arrangements for miscellaneous overhead cost will be similar to those for the production overhead cost, discussed in Chapter 8. As cash is spent, or liabilities are incurred, these are recorded as credits, releasing the cashier of a corresponding amount immediately, or recording his right to pay out the amount later in satisfaction of the liability. Cash discounts and bad debts reduce the debtors and release the accounting staff of the duty to collect an equivalent amount. Depreciation reduces the recorded value of the relevant assets and thus formally reduces the amount to be accounted for in respect of that asset. The expenses corresponding to these reductions in the business net assets are recorded as debits for which the departmental head is responsible. They form part of the profit and loss calculation, to which we now turn.

10

THE PROFIT AND LOSS STATEMENT

IN THE preceding chapters we have discussed the sales revenue, the cost of the goods sold, and the costs of departments not directly concerned with production. The sales budget shows the planned rise in the ownership claim which is conventionally assumed to occur at the moment of the increase in debtors as goods flow to the customer. The production budget, the work-in-progress budget and the finished goods budget, taken together, show and explain the corresponding planned fall in the ownership claim, measured conventionally by the costs of the production department, as the finished goods are sent out. The other departmental overhead cost budgets analyse the estimated decrease in the ownership claim as the result of the expenditure planned in the corresponding departments. The net change in the ownership claim from all these causes—the difference between the sales revenue and the costs—is the planned profit. It is not the budgeted *net* profit for the period however; there are certain other expenses not yet discussed. The remaining expenses include the salaries and fees of the departmental heads, the general manager, and the board (which are excluded from the overhead cost budgets because they are not under the control of the departmental heads), financial expenses (less financial revenues), dividends and taxation. It is characteristic of these expenses and revenues that they are likely to be planned directly by the board of directors.

Let us assume that the management salaries and fees for the year under review are £10,000. We combine this figure with the results of our earlier budget calculations in Table 10.1. We have first the budgeted gross profit—the sales revenue (Table 4.1) *less* the production cost of sales (Table 6.6)—and then, deducting management salaries and fees and the other overhead costs

(Tables 9.1, 9.2 and 9.3), the budgeted trading profit.[1] Table 10.1 is the first part of the budgeted profit and loss statement for the year.

One of the points of this table that attracts attention is the considerable variation in the budgeted trading profit from quarter to quarter. There is actually a trading loss of £1,960 in the second quarter, whereas in the third quarter there is a profit of £13,749. This is due to two factors. The first is the conventional definition of profit, which is only deemed to arise at the moment when the goods are sold and the sales value is recorded. Until then the goods are valued at (conventional) cost. This means that the planned gross profit tends to vary over time with the level of the sales revenue, as Table 10.1 shows. (We say 'tends', for a change in the mix of sales in favour of a product with, say, a lower ratio of standard production cost to sales price would cause gross profit to increase more than in proportion to an increase in sales revenue.) Secondly, the non-production overhead costs are exceptionally high in the June quarter as the result of the heavy advertising in that quarter (cf. Table 9.1). This heavy outlay converts the June quarter gross profit into a trading loss.

When the budget is interpreted it is necessary to remember that the heavy advertising outlay is probably part of the cost of securing sales in the September quarter as well as the June quarter. It could be argued reasonably that the advertising cost should have been spread over both quarters, even though the expense was incurred in the June quarter. The disadvantage of carrying this kind of adjustment very far is that it is usually in some degree arbitrary, and if there are many such items the trouble and time occupied in preparing the accounting reports may be considerable. In practice compromise is necessary: what is really important is that the budget, and the control of actual expenditure, should be interpreted having regard to the basis on which the figures are compiled. It is an important function of the controller's staff to interpret the figures on behalf of the management. This is not to say the data should not be made as clear as possible; but business itself is complex and all its com-

---

[1] In the legal company accounts directors' fees are not deducted in arriving at what is usually called the 'trading profit'; but here we are concerned with management data. The same is true of depreciation.

plications cannot be removed from the figures that describe and explain it.

TABLE 10.1

PROFIT AND LOSS BUDGET—TRADING
SECTION 19—

£

	Jan.–March	April–June	July–Sept.	Oct.–Dec.	Year
Sales revenue (Table 4.1) ..	85,500	103,000	129,500	82,000	400,000
Cost of sales (Table 6.6) ..	63,782	77,618	97,988	61,329	300,717
Gross profit ..	21,718	25,382	31,512	20,671	99,283
Selling and distribution cost (Table 9.1) ..	6,352	16,612	7,033	6,335	36,332
Research and development cost (Table 9.2) ..	5,100	5,100	5,100	5,100	20,400
General administration cost (Table 9.3) ..	3,130	3,130	3,130	3,161	12,551
General management salaries (page 129) ..	2,500	2,500	2,500	2,500	10,000
Miscellaneous overhead costs	17,082	27,342	17,763	17,096	79,283
Trading profit ..	4,636	−1,960	13,749	3,575	20,000

The remainder of the profit and loss budget is concerned with finance and taxation (Table 10.2). This table (which contains only annual figures) starts with the budgeted trading profit from Table 10.1. The next item is debenture interest. This is the cost of the long-term borrowing. It can be checked that the interest shown, £600, represents the contractual rate of interest, 4 per cent per annum, on the £15,000 debenture loan that appears in the opening balance sheet (Table 3.1). Then come the estimates of bank interest payable and investment income receivable. These are based upon expected rates of interest, the amounts planned to be borrowed or invested during the year, and the periods of the borrowing or investment. The planning of loans and investments, and therefore of the interest payments and receipts, is, however, dependent upon the contents of the finance budget, which will be discussed in Chapter 12. Here again, we have an example of the interdependence of the budgeting, for the finance budget itself depends on all the other budgets, including the profit and loss budget. As usual, we must assume that the final figures of each budget emerge as the result of a trial and error process, starting with first approximations in which the figures in the other budgets are assumed.

TABLE 10.2

PROFIT AND LOSS BUDGET—FINANCIAL SECTION 19—

	£	£
Trading profit (Table 10.1)		20,000
Less: debenture interest	600*	
bank interest	228	
	828	
Less: investment income	600*	
	—	228
Net profit before tax		19,772
Less: income tax (£9,103) and profits tax (£1,423) on this profit		10,526
Net profit after tax		9,246
Less: preference dividends (net of income tax)	288	
ordinary dividends (net of income tax) ..	2,200	
	—	2,488
Undistributed profit for year		6,758
Undistributed profit at January 1 (Table 3.1) ..		81,114
Total undistributed profit at December 31		87,872

*Of which £345 is the net payment (or receipt) and £255 the income tax payable thereon (*see* page 153).

Next come the anticipated income and profits taxes, determined by the expected profit and the current state of the law.

The remainder of the table shows the net profit, after tax, for the year, the dividends planned to be paid to the owners of the company—the shareholders—and the amount of profit to be left undistributed or 'ploughed-back' into the business for the year, to which is added the figure of undistributed profit at the beginning of the year as it appears in the opening balance sheet. The final figure is the total profit not distributed at the end of the year, and will appear as part of the ownership claim in the budgeted closing balance sheet.

The payment of interest on debentures and of dividends on shares are rather different in nature, though both represent in a sense the cost of long term finance provided to the company. The interest on the debentures is a legal liability which can be sued for in the courts if it is not paid regularly. The dividends to shareholders are payable to the people who are nominally part owners of the business if, and only if, sufficient profit has (at some time) been earned to meet these dividends and has not already been distributed or formally converted (by the legal process of 'capitalization') into permanent capital. The payments to the shareholders are also at the discretion of the directors though if the preference dividend, which is a fixed annual amount, is 'cumulative', the ordinary shareholders can receive nothing until any arrears of the agreed preference dividend are paid. The ordinary dividend is the amount which the directors have decided to pay to the ordinary or 'equity' shareholders—those with the residual claim. All the dividends are described as 'net of income tax' because under British income tax law the company pays tax on all its profit 'on behalf of its shareholders' and is entitled to recover tax from the contractual amount payable on the preference dividends. (The ordinary dividend is also called 'net' but as the ordinary shareholders have the residual interest this has no significance for the company. It has, however, a tax significance for the individual shareholders.)

The budgets of Tables 10.1 and 10.2 together explain the expected change in the net claim of the owners against the business as the result of the current business operations. Changes in the amount of this claim may also arise from payments of additional capital into the business, or withdrawals of capital, by the owners, but these will not affect the profit and loss statements.[1]

---

[1] Withdrawals of ownership capital from companies are only possible by certain types of legal procedure.

Profit and loss control

The control of the profit and loss position of the business is largely obtained through the control of the individual components which we have discussed in earlier chapters, and at the beginning of this chapter. It is of the nature of the expenses and revenues mentioned in this chapter that variances of the actual from the budgeted figures will be relatively easy to analyse: in the example that we are examining the only figures which are likely to vary seriously from the budgeted ones for reasons other than deliberate management decisions are the investment income, the bank interest and the tax. Variations in the debenture interest payments or in the dividend payments will be the result of deliberate management policy, and will not require further explanation. Apart from changes in the law, tax will vary with changes in the net profit itself; if the change in the profit is explained the change in the tax will be automatically explained as well.

The double-entry accounting records and the internal accounting control raise no important points of principle that have not been met already.

Interpretation of the profit and loss statements

The profit and loss budget summarizes the result of the various activities of the business. Its preparation is also part of the process of checking the mutual consistency of all the budgets. The profit and loss budgets and accounts together also provide a general control over the operation of the business as a whole. The successful running of a business in the longer run requires that an appropriate level of net profit shall be achieved, though it is not easy to determine what this level should be; this depends upon the nature of the business. In private enterprise, however, it may be said as a broad generalization that the object is to ensure that the annual rate of profit upon the market value of the resources used in the business (i.e. the value of the net assets) shall on average not be below the rate of profit that could be earned by using them for some other purpose. This is subject to the qualification that some businesses are more risky and uncertain than others and that higher profits will be required from these. In a State industry the object may be to earn a certain prescribed level of profit after paying interest on the finance

It reflects the responsibility of the purchasing organization. The latter may be a section of the production manager's department; this is what we assumed for our business in Chapter 1. This need not be so in every business, however, particularly if the nature of the business is such that the purchasing requires the exercise of special expertise; in such a case there may be an independent purchasing manager. The physical control of the material in store may be in the hands of the production department; sometimes however the controller may be responsible.

In practice this budget may cover materials and components to be used not only in the production department but in other departments of the business: the research and development department will probably use many kinds of materials, the sales department and the administration will use stationery, office machinery spares, and so on. We shall illustrate here only the budget relating to materials for production, since this will be sufficient to establish the principles. (We can assume if we like that so far as other departments have used materials these have been budgeted as part of the overhead expenses of those departments discussed in Chapter 9, and that no stocks are held.)

The materials budget is built up by considering the materials (including components) that will be required for the planned production programme, as discussed in Chapter 5, and the minimum stocks which it is thought desirable to hold. To the value held at the beginning of each period (e.g. as shown in the opening balance sheet in Table 3.1) is added the value of the planned purchases (which will tally with the increase in liabilities to creditors shown below). From the sum of the opening stock and the purchases is deducted the value of the amounts expected to be used during the period. (These figures tally with the material usages of Table 5.2.) We are left with the estimated value of stock at the end of the period. This will appear in the closing balance sheet. The general form of the budget is indicated in Table 11.1.

We have discussed earlier the general problems that arise in calculating the amounts of raw materials that will be used in production. The estimation of the stocks that should be carried at different times raises the same kind of problems as were discussed on page 57 with respect to finished goods stocks. On the one hand

TABLE 11.1

MATERIALS BUDGET 19—

	Jan.–March	April–June	£ July–Sept.	Oct.–Dec.	Year
Opening stock (Table 3.1) ..	8,245	9,032	7,026	7,091	8,245
Purchases ..	51,437	51,042	41,466	43,405	187,350
	59,682	60,074	48,492	50,496	195,595
Issues (Table 5.2)	50,650	53,048	41,401	42,251	187,350
Closing stock ..	9,032	7,026	7,091	8,245	8,245

must be balanced the disadvantage of running out of stock when it is required for production, which may sometimes cause serious loss. Against this risk must be balanced the facts that every additional pound's worth of stock in the business is absorbing additional finance, involving an interest cost, and that there are storage expenses and risks of deterioration. Furthermore, the greater the stock that is held, the greater will be the loss to the company should there be a downward change in prices (or, of course, the gain if prices should rise). In most businesses the estimation of the correct levels of different kinds of stock is done by intuition, rule of thumb, or intelligent guesswork, but as noted on page 58, mathematical methods of estimating the best levels can sometimes help.

Budgetary control will, as usual, be maintained by comparing the value of actual stocks held with the budgeted amounts.

The stock of materials held must be recorded in the formal accounts on the basis of some kind of conventional valuation. Of the methods available, that based on standard pricing seems most convenient. As stock is acquired the amounts are valued at the standard price and recorded. If the actual prices happen to be the same as the standard prices, the amounts so recorded will be equal to the amounts entered at the same time as due to the creditors who supplied the materials. In practice, however, the purchase prices are unlikely to tally exactly with the standard prices and the differences, adverse or favourable, must be reported as material price variances, which in some sense record the success or failure of the purchasing department to achieve the standards set.

The physical care of materials stock will be arranged by laying down a procedure for the receipt and care of goods as they arrive. Certain employees will be authorized to receive the goods and sign the receipt, the goods will then be passed to an inspection department with the object of finding out whether they are up to the specification in the original order, and from the inspection department they will be passed to the care of the storekeeper. Once they are in his care they will not be issued without formal authority. Backing up this physical control are the formal double-entry accounts which state the value of stock of each kind that is (or ought to be) in the store at any particular time and which can, if desired, be checked by a physical count.

These stock accounts will be built up by arranging for all movements of materials inside the organization from one area of responsibility to another to be reported to the accounting department. For example, the inspection department reports when the materials move to the control of the storekeeper. The storekeeper reports when they are issued. The report of the inspection department also advises the accounting department that the goods are in order and that therefore payment can be made for them. The accounting department will make arrangements to ensure that no liability is created in the accounting records unless the correct goods have arrived: the bill from the supplier is checked against the inspection report, the report from the store that the goods have been received, and, to provide a check against the receipt of goods which have not been properly ordered by the purchasing department, the record of the original order. The information on the bill (invoice) from the supplier can be used to set up the entry in the creditor's account and, in conjunction with the record of standard prices, the entries in the stock account and the raw material price variance account.

This procedure and record-keeping will be carried out by the accounting department in close co-operation with the production, planning and purchasing organizations. It is not possible to state in general terms exactly how the various duties will be allocated. Action which in one business would be taken in the accounting department—for example, checking the reports of goods received against the orders—might in another be done in the materials planning department. All that has been attempted here is to sketch the general nature of the arrangements. The nature of the actual records and the way in which the different notifications are transmitted will vary a good deal.

Debtors

We now turn to the debtors budget (Table 11.2). This budget reflects the responsibility of the accounting department for the preservation and collection of the debts which arise from the sales department's activities. We start in row 1, column 1, with the amount that will be owing on January 1. To this we add the estimated sales for the March quarter, which have already been discussed in connection with the sales budget. We then estimate the cash that will be received from debtors during the quarter. This will depend upon the average period of credit allowed. Debtors who pay before a specified time may be allowed a cash discount and a deduction must therefore be made of the estimated discount that will be taken. A deduction is necessary also for estimated bad debts. The balance remaining is the amount of good debts at the end of the quarter. (We assume that the sales figure is net, i.e. that it allows for any returns from customers in respect of unsuitable goods and any allowances for poor quality.) We make similar calculations for each quarter. The opening balance in January agrees with the figure in the opening balance sheet (Table 3.1). The cash received will appear in the cash budget, as we shall see later. The discounts and bad debts have appeared as part of the expense shown in the selling and distribution cost budget (Table 9.1). The balance at December 31 will be part of the estimated closing balance sheet.

The accounting records will, as usual, be arranged so that the actual figures can be reported and compared with the budget figures. In practice it is likely that they will be reported to the controller, and perhaps to the general management, weekly: the flow of cash into the business in the near future depends to a large extent upon the level of debts; an undue growth in these caused by slow payment, or an unusual loss through bad debts, are the kind of events that must be brought very early to the attention of the management.

We have discussed in Chapter 4 the kind of procedures that will be set up to ensure that the sales figures debited to the customers' accounts are, as far as possible, correct. The next step in the chain

TABLE 11.2

DEBTORS BUDGET 19—

	Jan.–March	April–June	July–Sept.	Oct.–Dec.	Year
			£		
Opening balance (Table 3.1) ..	35,760	41,147	60,057	46,992	35,760
Sales (Table 4.1) ..	85,500	103,000	129,500	82,000	400,000
	121,260	144,147	189,557	128,992	435,760
Cash	79,407	83,375	141,694	88,062	392,538
Cash discounts (Table 9.1) ..	206	215	371	200	992
Bad debts (Table 9.1) ..	500	500	500	500	2,000
	80,113	84,090	142,565	88,762	395,530
Closing balance	41,147	60,057	46,992	40,230	40,230

of internal control is to ensure as far as possible that these balances are only reduced when payment has been received, or when a duly authorized deduction, e.g. for cash discount, has been allowed. The debtors' records will be kept by different employees from those who keep the cash records or the records of discounts, bad debts and allowances. The debtors' control account, which records the transactions and debts due in total, is compiled through different channels and by different persons from the individual debtors' accounts, of which it is a summary, and against which it is frequently checked. These arrangements are intended to ensure that unless error or fraud is committed by at least two people it will be revealed by disagreement in the accounts. For example, the person in charge of the debtors' accounts might agree privately with one of the debtors to enter in his account an unauthorized credit recording that he had paid. This reduction in a recorded asset would not be offset by an equivalent reduction in a liability, or by a recorded expense (fall in ownership claim), nor would the summary control account now agree with the sum of the individual debtors' accounts; there would therefore be two arithmetical disagreements when the accounts were proved and these would be investigated. Again, the possibility that the debtor may not receive a bill, and the balance to the debit of his account be deliberately left permanently outstanding, is dealt with by arranging that the bills are sent out by a different person from that responsible for the debtors' accounts. The latter would notice eventually that there was an old balance which had not been paid and enquiries would be made. Furthermore, there would be a routine inspection of balances for old debts. This is not an exhaustive description of the system likely to be operating; but it illustrates the principles on which the internal accounting control depends.

Creditors

This budget bears the same relation to the suppliers of the company that the debtors budget bears to the customers, and reflects another area of responsibility of the accounting organization. The form that it might take is illustrated in table 11.3. We have, in row 1, column 1, the amount that is expected to be owing to suppliers on January 1. We add to this the planned purchases of materials in the March quarter. We deduct the cash that is expected to be paid to suppliers during the quarter. We are left with the amount that will, if all goes according to plan, be owing to suppliers at the end of the quarter. The estimate of cash payments in the quarter will depend upon the period of credit that will be obtained from suppliers, and the dates of the purchases. If it is the custom of the trade for suppliers to give

TABLE 11.3

CREDITORS BUDGET 19—

£

	Jan.–March	April–June	July–Sept.	Oct.–Dec.	Year
Opening balance (Table 3.1) ..	14,000	17,625	15,486	14,182	14,000
Purchases (Table 11.1) ..	51,437	51,042	41,466	43,405	187,350
	65,437	68,667	56,952	57,587	201,350
Cash	47,812	53,181	42,770	42,157	185,920
Closing balance	17,625	15,486	14,182	15,430	15,430

cash discounts for early payment, a deduction will be made for any of these that are expected to be taken. In our example we have assumed that there are no cash discounts. The opening balance, the creditors at the beginning of the year, will agree with the figure in the opening balance sheet (Table 3.1). The figures in the second row, the purchases, are the same as those that appear in row 2 of the materials budget (Table 11.1). The payments of cash we shall find later in the cash budget. The closing balance at the end of each quarter is the opening balance at the beginning of the next quarter. The closing balance at the end of the year will be part of the estimated final balance sheet.

As with the debtors, the actual figures will be reported to the controller, and probably the general management, as they are obtained from the accounting records, probably weekly. Changes in these figures, too, can affect the financial position of the company very rapidly. For example, if there are heavy purchases over and above the original budget estimates in a particular month, the cash outgoing at the end of the period of credit granted by the suppliers will be correspondingly raised. It is very important that any change of this type should be brought rapidly to the notice of those responsible for the financial control, so that they can ensure the cash needed is available.

The report of the actual figures will be a summary of the creditors' control account—the account that summarises the individual creditors' accounts in the formal double-entry system. As with the debtors' control account, the balance is continually checked against the balances on the individual creditors' accounts. The accounts are so arranged that the collection of the data for the summary control account is independent of the collection of the data for the individual creditors' accounts. Both sets of records are maintained independently of the persons responsible for the payment of the cash and for the original authentication of the liability for goods received.

One of the main objects of the control of creditors' accounts is to ensure as far as possible that no cash payments are made to unauthorized persons, and in particular that no unauthorized liabilities are recorded in the creditors' accounts which could then lead to a payment of cash to a person apparently entitled to receive it— i.e. to ensure that cash payments which are recorded against a

F

particular creditor are in fact in reduction of a correctly existing liability which has already been approved.

Internal control: an example

We shall conclude this chapter by demonstrating the general principles of internal control, showing how it might operate with respect to creditors. Suppose that a clerk falsely prepares documents suggesting that a liability exists towards a friend of his outside the business, by fraudulent misrepresentation obtains approval from a departmental head for payment of the bill, and passes it to the cashier for the normal procedure of cash payment to operate. If there were no other control, the cheque would be drawn and signed on the strength of the approved documents, and the money would be paid to the fraudulent person outside the business.

Let us now examine what will happen in the accounting records. The cash payment must be recorded. This is the only way in which the cashier can show that he is no longer responsible for the amount in question. The amount will appear, therefore, as a credit (i.e. a reduction) in the cash account. There must, however, be a corresponding debit in the accounts or they will fail to balance. (Indeed, the routine will normally be so arranged that the total of cash credits in any given day must be arithmetically agreed with the total of debits to the various accounts; this agreement will not be the responsibility of the cashier himself but of some other person.) If the fraud is not to be discovered at once an unauthorized debit must therefore find its way into the accounts.

There are then two possibilities. The debit may be recorded as an expense, that is as a reduction in the ownership claim. If this happens the fraud may never be discovered—unless it is unearthed as the result of an investigation into the level of expense, e.g. to explain a variance from budget. The false 'expense' along with all the others will be summarized at the end of a given accounting period and will enter into the net profit or loss for the period. For this reason special care has to be taken of any debits to accounts that do not record assets or liabilities.

The other possibility is that a false debit may be made to an asset account (increasing the asset) or to a liability account (reducing the liability). In the former case an amount which has to be safeguarded, and which is under someone's control, has been increased. For example, if the amount is recorded as an additional debt from some person, then whoever is responsible for the group of accounts in which this debt is recorded will take steps sooner or later to see it is collected. It will then be discovered that it is not a normal business debt and the original fraud will no doubt come to light on investigation. If the false debit is made to an account that represents some other kind of asset, the person who is responsible for that account will sooner or later, if the system is working well, find that the debit balance on the account does not tally with the physical facts. For example, if the amount is debited to the summary control account recording the value of the stock of raw materials there will be a disagreement between this account and the sum of the balances in the detailed stock accounts.

Alternatively, if the amount is debited to a liability account (i.e. the liability is reduced) the result of this will be that the creditor in question will be paid less than the amount which was originally standing to his credit, he will protest, and again there will be an investigation.

In the final chapter we shall discuss the budgeting of the cash flows of the business. We shall then conclude with the budgeted balance sheet at the end of the year, together with the budgets of the tax transactions, the dividends owing to shareholders at various times, and the changes in fixed assets and investments, which are needed to complete the link between the opening and closing balance sheets.

12

FINANCE

THE finance budget is extremely important. It records the planned receipts and payments of money on which depends the 'liquidity'—the availability of money—of the business. It is not possible to plan the conduct of the business properly unless a reasonably good estimate of the cash inflow and outflow is available. In the absence of such an estimate the business runs the risk of being unable to pay its debts as they fall due, or of being unable to maintain the planned level of activity, e.g. because cash is not available when needed to pay wages and other outgoings; or, on the other hand, it may find itself with a cash balance in excess of current needs which is not earning interest and for which a satisfactory investment cannot be found quickly.

It is true that there are no unambiguous rules by which to determine whether the level of the cash balance in any particular firm at any given time is correct. This is a matter of judgement and experience. The judgement, however, should be well-informed.

It is convenient to divide the estimates of cash receipts and payments into two sections. We shall call the first section the operating cash budget. This deals with the receipts and payments that arise out of the normal recurring activities whose revenue and costs are summarized in the trading section of the profit and loss budget (Table 10.1). The second section, which we shall call the finance budget, is concerned with the cash inflow and outflow of the company as a whole. It has particular reference to the way in which additional finance may have to be raised from outside the business, the expenditure of money on long term investment projects, and the payment of dividends and interest, which are closely related to the way in which the outside finance is obtained. It deals with receipts of cash from the liquidation of investments or other assets, and payments of cash representing the temporary or longer term investment of money not required in the current operation of the business. It is also convenient to include in this budget the tax payments. One of its components is the net surplus or deficit shown by the operating cash budget.

Operating cash budget

The figures in the operating cash budget (Table 12.1) are implied by the budgets we have already discussed. If the table is examined it will be seen that each figure has already appeared in a previous table. This can be shown by reference to column 5. If we take first

TABLE 12.1

OPERATING CASH BUDGET 19—

£

	Jan.–March	April–June	July–Sept.	Oct.–Dec.	Year
Receipts:					
Sales (Table 11.2) ..	79,407	83,375	141,694	88,062	392,538
Payments:					
Production materials purchases (Table 11.3) ..	47,812	53,181	42,770	42,157	185,920
Production labour (Table 5.3) ..	25,986	26,450	22,507	23,807	98,750
Production general expense (Table 5.4)*	2,129	1,742	1,629	2,000	7,500
Selling and distribution cost (Table 9.1)* ..	5,646	15,897	6,162	5,635	33,340
Research and development cost (Table 9.2)* ..	4,710	4,710	4,710	4,710	18,840
General administration cost (Table 9.3)* ..	2,791	2,791	2,791	2,822	11,195
General management salaries and fees (Table 10.1) ..	2,500	2,500	2,500	2,500	10,000
Total payments ..	91,574	107,271	83,069	83,631	365,545
Operating surplus	−12,167	−23,896	58,625	4,431	26,993

* Excluding 'non-cash' items: depreciation, cash discounts, bad debts *see* text).

the sales receipts of £392,538, we find that these agree with the total of cash received from debtors shown in the debtors budget (Table 11.2). The first cash payment, £185,920, is the amount paid to trade creditors from whom materials and components have been bought, and appears in the trade creditors budget (Table 11.3). The next figure is £98,750 for production labour. This agrees with Table 5.3.

The next four cash payments, production general expense, selling and distribution, research and development and general administration cost, can be reconciled with figures in the corresponding expense budgets. They are, however, less than the total expense of these budgets: depreciation, and (in the selling cost budget) cash discounts and bad debts, are costs, being reductions in the value of assets, but they are not cash outlays. The value sacrificed is either a deduction from the value of fixed assets (in the case of depreciation), or a deduction from the debtors (in the case of cash discounts and bad debts).

That depreciation is not a cash outlay is particularly significant: once equipment has been bought it may help to earn revenue for a number of years during which no part of the incoming cash need be spent on renewal or replacement, and hence it is available for the time being to finance expansion or the reduction of debt. Thus, the cash becoming available from the current operation of the business is in general greater than the profit, whose calculation is net of a depreciation allowance. On the other hand, the finance budget must, as we shall see, allow for cash outlays on new equipment, and these may in a given year be greater than the depreciation for that year.

It may be noted that the cash payments on wages are here shown to be identical with the production cost of wages. This implies that there are no amounts owing at the end of each quarter to employees in respect of wages not yet paid, or that if there are such amounts they are the same at the beginning and end of the quarter. This will not always be true. The work is done before the wages are paid; hence, when the payment of wages does not coincide with the final date of the accounting year it will be necessary to include as part of the wage cost (and therefore of the value of work-in-progress) the cost of labour done but not yet paid for.

The employees will then appear as creditors and the changes in the amounts owing to them can be included in a special creditors budget. The same point applies to deductions from wages for income tax, etc.: until these are paid over to the tax authorities, etc., the latter will be creditors. We have similarly assumed that in the case of the production general expense and the other overhead costs (except depreciation and the other 'non-cash' expenses) the value outgoing is coincident with the cash payment. In fact many such outlays reflect, in the first instance, the creation of a liability, and the cash payment comes later, then representing merely the surrender of an asset and the extinction of a liability—a change in asset structure. There may also be cash payments to creditors in respect of expenses incurred in an earlier period. In practice it would be necessary, therefore, to adjust for creditors under nearly all the expense classifications and this would require separate creditors budgets. The principle of this adjustment has been demonstrated in the creditors budget in Table 11.3.

Total cash payments in Table 12.1 in respect of the above items, plus the general administration salaries and fees, amount to £365,545. The difference between this sum and the cash received from debtors is the budgeted operating cash surplus of £26,993.

One of the important points brought out by Table 12.1 is that only in the third and fourth quarters is there a surplus. The surplus for the whole year is the difference between the surplus in those quarters and the deficit in the first two quarters. Some kind of seasonal pattern of cash receipts and payments of this kind is common in business and follows from the pattern of sales revenue and of expenses. The months of cash deficit will not, however, necessarily tally with the months in which the conventional accounting practice shows a loss in the profit and loss statement, because changes in assets other than cash, and in liabilities, can also affect the profit.

The net surplus in Table 12.1, £26,993, represents the cash expected to be generated during the year as a result of the current business activities. Before the general management can come to a decision about the final approval of all the budgets they must decide whether this net surplus is consistent with the general financial planning of the business. We now, therefore, turn to the finance budget.

Finance budget

The pattern of the finance budget is indicated in Table 12.2. We start in January with the opening cash balance—the cash at bank shown in the opening balance sheet. To this we add (or deduct) the expected operating cash surplus (or deficit) from Table 12.1. Then

TABLE 12.2

FINANCE BUDGET 19—

£

	Jan.–March	April–June	July–Sept.	Oct.–Dec.	Year
Receipts:					
Opening cash balance (Table 3.1)	17,000	1,240	−24,215	6,275	17,000
Operating surplus (Table 12.1)	−12,167	−23,896	58,625	4,431	26,993
Investment income (Table 10.2) ..	57	—	—	288	345
	4,890	−22,656	34,410	10,994	44,338
Payments:					
Debenture interest (Table 10.2) ..	—	172	—	173	345
Bank interest (Table 10.2) ..	—	143	85	—	228
Tax (Table 12.5) ..	7,000	1,100	—	—	8,100
Preference dividends (Table 12.6) ..	—	144	—	144	288
Ordinary dividends (Table 12.6) ..	1,650	—	550	—	2,200
Capital expenditure (Table 12.3) ..	—	—	2,500	3,000	5,500
	8,650	1,559	3,135	3,317	16,661
Surplus finance (+) or deficit to be financed (−)	−3,760	−24,215	31,275	7,677	27,677
Sale (+) or purchase (−) of investments (Table 12.9) ..	5,000	—	−25,000	—	−20,000
Closing cash balance (+) or overdraft (−)	1,240	−24,215	6,275	7,677	7,677

The long term finance budget

The long term finance budget of the business (which we shall not illustrate here) comprises a series of finance budgets of the type we have been examining, extended into the future. As in the current year, every one of the figures in this budget is inter-connected with every other one and all the years are interdependent. The budget is also related functionally to what has already happened in the year we are considering and in previous years since these determine the resources and environment of the future. The long term finance budget is relevant in connection with all longer term financing plans, including the issue of debentures or shares, since it is by constructing a budget of this kind that the future annual amounts that will be available for interest or dividend payments are estimated.

The drafting of this budget is really a statement of the longer term assumptions on which all the current budgets, and in particular the capital expenditure and finance budgets, are based. It will seldom be possible—or sensible—to make such close estimations of the various constituents as were made for the current year's budget. This is especially applicable to the estimated operating cash surpluses for future years. Such estimates as are made will generally be based on the extrapolation of sales revenues, and costs, into the future, with adjustments for expected changes in price levels and for other expected economic changes in the conditions of business. The result can never be 'correct'. Nevertheless some approximate framework for thinking about the future is necessary.

This is particularly relevant when the board are planning the making and financing of large-scale capital expenditure. Such plans have to be converted into flows of cash that can be incorporated into the long term finance budget. The effect of the new assets resulting from the expenditure on the operating cash surpluses of future years must be gauged: it is from the increase in these surpluses that the capital expenditure must eventually be recouped and the interest or dividends on the new finance provided. The pattern of the initial cash outlay on the new assets must be planned; the additional finance that will be needed to pay for them and for the extra stocks of materials and work-in-progress that will be carried must be worked out, and the manner and timing of raising it decided; this in turn will determine the future payments of interest and dividends to be met out of the increased operating cash flow.

The long term finance budget summarizes in a sense the whole economic aspect of the business. It implies a whole mass of guesses, estimates and assumptions about the conduct of the business. It expresses the overall policy plans of the board of directors. It provides in short a symbolic picture of the business capable of being broken down into very great detail in the current year and implying a correspondingly detailed breakdown in the later years, even though this may not be practically possible before these years are approached. Once such a budget has been drafted the management have a general plan on which they can base their thinking.

It is essential for the proper understanding and use of this kind of statement that the general interdependence of the business in space and time which we discussed in Chapter 1 should be understood. In a certain sense every figure which appears in any of the budgets we have discussed depends in some respects upon all the other figures in the budgets. In the final analysis the budgets have to be settled together, both for a given year and for the number of years into the future for which it is considered worthwhile forecasting.

Long term finance

The considerations that will sway a board of directors when deciding whether to raise longer term finance by one means rather than another, by debentures rather than by preference shares, by fixed interest securities rather than by ordinary shares, cannot be more than touched on here. The issue of debentures is regarded in law as borrowing. A legal liability is created. Henceforth the company will have to pay the interest annually if it is to avoid legal action being taken against it, and will have to find the money to repay the debenture loan at the time when this has been promised. There is no way of avoiding this without the consent of the debenture holders. An issue of preference shares gives the directors more flexibility. If in any given year the liquidity position is bad, or the profit is low, the payment of dividend can be postponed without immediate serious consequences, though, as we have already noted, this may mean that the preference shareholders will

TABLE 12.4

BUDGETED BALANCE SHEET—DECEMBER 31 19—

	£	£
Long and Medium Term Liabilities:		
Debenture carrying interest at 4% p.a. (Table 3.1)	15,000	
Future income tax (Table 12.5)	9,103	
Current Liabilities:		
Trade creditors (Table 11.3)	15,430	
Income tax and profits tax (Table 12.5)	9,423	
Dividends to be paid to shareholders (Table 12.6)	1,650	
	26,503	
Total Liabilities		50,606
Ordinary Shareholders:		
Capital paid in (Table 3.1)	12,000	
Profits earned and not distributed (Table 10.2)	87,872	
	99,872	
Preference Shareholders:		
Capital paid in carrying a cumulative dividend of 5% p.a. (Table 3.1)	10,000	
Total Shareholders' Claims		109,872
Total Claims		160,478

	£	£
Fixed Assets:		
Land and buildings (Table 12.7)		29,504
Plant, machinery and equipment (Table 12.8)		25,678
		55,182
Current Assets:		
Stocks:		
Raw materials (Table 11.1)	8,245	
Work-in-progress (Table 6.5)	12,410	
Finished goods (Table 6.6)	11,734	
	32,389	
Trade debtors (Table 11.2)	40,230	
Investments (Table 12.9)	25,000	
Cash (Table 12.2)	7,677	
		105,296
Total Assets		160,478

This balance sheet is not drafted for legal purposes under the Companies Act.

convenient at this stage to introduce budgets for the changes in the taxation liabilities, the dividends owing to shareholders, the fixed assets and investments.

The closing balance sheet is shown in Table 12.4. Each figure in it can be related to one of the other budgets, or directly to the opening balance sheet.

We start with the liabilities. The first figure is the debenture loan of £15,000. This is unchanged during the year and is taken directly from the opening balance sheet.

Next we come to the income tax payable one year after December 31, £9,103, and, under current liabilities, the income tax and profits tax payable soon after December 31, £9,423. The derivation of these figures is explained in Table 12.5. This table may not be easy for a novice to follow. The secret of puzzling it out is to remember it is really no more than a reconciliation of liabilities at the beginning and end of the year with (*a*) new liabilities arising during the year (which are the counterpart of expenses in the profit and loss budget) and (*b*) reduction of liabilities effected by cash payments (which are in the finance budget). Remember that the expense which goes in the profit and loss statement arises when the liability is recognized (fall in shareholders' claim, rise in liability) and that the cash payment then merely extinguishes the liability (fall in asset, fall in liability). The relationship implied in the table between the dates of payment of the taxes and the profits on which they are paid is a matter of tax law that cannot be discussed here; it may be noted, however, that in this respect income tax differs from profits tax. The actual tax figures used have been chosen arbitrarily, though the tax on the current year's profit bears the approximate relation to that profit to be expected at the time of writing.

The figure in Table 12.4 for trade creditors, £15,430, is obtained from the budget in Table 11.3.

The ordinary dividend to be paid to shareholders, £1,650, is explained in Table 12.6.

The shareholders' capital, ordinary and preference, has not changed during the year and appears as it did in Table 3.1. The shareholders' claim in respect of retained profit, £87,872, is the final figure of Table 10.2.

TABLE 12.5

BUDGET OF INCOME TAX AND
PROFITS TAX TRANSACTIONS 19..

	£
At January 1 the company owes:	
for income tax on the profits of the previous year but one payable at once	7,000
for profits tax on the profits of the previous year and payable within the next year	1,100
these two are therefore current liabilities at opening balance sheet date (Table 3.1)	8,100
income tax on the profits of the previous year and payable on January 1 one year later (Table 3.1)	8,000
Total tax liabilities, current and deferred, at opening balance sheet date are therefore	16,100
Of these, the current income and profits tax to be paid in this year (Table 12.2) are	8,100
Leaving the current income tax liability at December 31 at ..	8,000
To this is added the profits tax estimated to be payable next year on this year's profit (Table 10.2)	1,423
Giving the estimated total current tax liability at December 31 (Table 12.4)	9,423
The estimated income tax on the current year's profit (Table 10.2) is	9,103
Add to this the tax deducted from the debenture interest when this is paid to the holders, which must be accounted for to the Revenue authorities (£600 in Table 10.2 *less* £345 in Table 12.2)	255
	9,358
Deduct from this the tax withheld from the investment income received which has thus already been paid (£600 in Table 10.2 *less* £345 in Table 12.2)	255
Leaving the deferred or future tax payable one year later (Table 12.4)	9,103

On the assets side we start with land and buildings. The relationship between the figures in the opening and closing balance sheets is analysed in Table 12.7. The following table, 12.8, analyses similarly the changes in the plant, machinery and equipment. The counter-part of the depreciation which formed part of the overhead costs of Chapters 5 and 9 appears as a reduction in the value of fixed assets. In both groups of assets there are additions to be made corresponding to the cash outlay in the capital expenditure budget.

All figures classified as current assets have appeared as parts of budgets already discussed except the investments; these are explained in Table 12.9.

If the reader were now prepared to make a careful check through the book, summarizing the budgeted accounting values of assets, liabilities and shareholders' claims, at December 31 (where no change is expected during the year, this is the value in the opening balance sheet), he would find that they have all now been accounted for. The fact that our balance sheet does indeed balance is the proof. Though this proof is not conclusive (since compensating errors do occur) it is strong evidence in favour of the proposition that our calculations are at least arithmetically consistent.

TABLE 12.6

BUDGET OF CHANGES IN DIVIDENDS OWING TO SHAREHOLDERS 19—

	£	£
Owing at January 1, final ordinary dividend for preceding year (Table 3.1)		1,650
Add: preference dividends payable in respect of year's profit (Table 10.2)	288	
ordinary dividends payable in respect of year's profit (Table 10.2)	2,200	
		2,488
		4,138
Less: cash to be paid—		
preference dividends (Table 12.2)	288	
ordinary dividends (Table 12.2)	2,200	
		2,488
Owing at December 31, final ordinary dividend for current year (Table 12.4)		1,650

All dividends are payable net of tax.

TABLE 12.7

BUDGET OF CHANGES IN LAND AND BUILDINGS 19—

	£	£
Balance sheet value at January 1 (Table 3.1)		27,500
Cost of budgeted additions (Table 12.3)		3,000
		30,500
Budgeted depreciation—		
research and development cost (Table 9.2) ..	840	
general administration cost (Table 9.3)	156	
		996
Balance sheet value at December 31 (Table 12.4) ..		29,504

TABLE 12.8

BUDGET OF CHANGES IN PLANT, MACHINERY AND EQUIPMENT 19—

	£	£
Balance sheet value at January 1 (Table 3.1)		31,500
Cost of budgeted additions (Table 12.3)		2,500
		34,000
Budgeted depreciation—		
production general expense (Table 5.4)	6,402	
research and development cost (Table 9.2) ..	720	
general administration cost (Table 9.3)	1,200	
		8,322
Balance sheet value at December 31 (Table 12.4) ..		25,678

TABLE 12.9

BUDGET OF CHANGES IN INVESTMENTS 19—

	£
Balance sheet value at January 1 (Table 3.1)	5,000
Less: sales in March quarter (Table 12.2)	5,000
	—
Add: purchases in September quarter (Table 12.2)	25,000
Balance sheet value at December 31 (Table 12.4)	25,000

167

SHORT READING LIST

General introduction to business and its problems

R. S. Edwards and H. Townsend, *Business Enterprise* (Macmillan, London).

F. W. Paish, *Business Finance* (Pitman, London).

Edith Tilton Penrose, *The Theory of the Growth of the Firm* (Blackwell, Oxford).

H. B. Rose, *The Economic Background to Investment* (Cambridge University Press).

Methods and practice of budgeting and costing

D. Solomons (Ed.), *Studies in Costing* (Sweet & Maxwell, London).
This is strongly recommended. A large part requires no previous knowledge of accounting.

I. W. Keller, *Management Accounting for Profit Control* (McGraw-Hill, New York).

A. Willsmore, *Business Budgets and Budgetary Control* (Pitman, London).

Institute of Cost and Works Accountants, *An Introduction to Budgetary Control, Standard Costing, Material Control and Production Control* (The Institute, London).
Certain parts of these books (Willsmore is an exception) require for complete understanding some knowledge of general accounting, such as can be obtained from Grant, or Robnett, Hill and Beckett, mentioned below, both of which include sections on budgeting and costing.

Ezra Solomon (Ed.), *The Management of Corporate Capital* (University of Chicago).
This collection of studies deals, at varying levels of difficulty, with important problems that arise in capital budgeting and financial planning.

The use and interpretation of accounting data

R. J. Chambers, *Financial Management* (Sweet & Maxwell, London).

J. H. Clemens, *Balance Sheets and the Lending Banker* (Europa, London).

Though addressed primarily to a banking audience, this book is a useful general guide to the analysis and interpretation of balance sheets and profit and loss accounts.

R. A. Foulke, *Practical Financial Statement Analysis* (McGraw-Hill, New York).

General accounting techniques and financial accounting

W. T. Baxter (Ed.), *Studies in Accounting* (Sweet & Maxwell London).

R. J. Chambers, *Accounting and Action* (Law Book Co. of Australasia, Sydney).

L. Goldberg and V. R. Hill, *The Elements of Accounting* (Melbourne University Press and Cambridge University Press).

E. L. Grant, *Basic Accounting and Cost Accounting* (McGraw-Hill, New York).

R. H. Robnett, T. M. Hill and J. A. Beckett, *Accounting: A Management Approach* (Irwin, Chicago).

The history of accounting

A. C. Littleton and B. S. Yamey (Eds.), *Studies in the History of Accounting* (Sweet & Maxwell, London).

Accounting terminology is not standardized, even within national boundaries; and there are differences between the usages of different countries. This is not a serious problem, but is one the careful reader will bear in mind.